another world is possible

---

new world disorder

conversations in a time of terror

© 2001 Subway & Elevated Press
All rights reserved
ISBN 0-9666469-6-7
Distributed by New Mouth from the Dirty South
To order copies of this book, send $12 per book to:
New Mouth from the Dirty South
PO Box 19742
New Orleans, LA 70179
or order online at:
www.newmouthfromthedirtysouth.com
Discounts available for orders of ten or more copies
books@newmouthfromthedirtysouth.com
Printed in the United States of America on recycled paper
Book design by Amy Woloszyn: awolo1@hotmail.com

forward

Everyone who witnessed the violence in New York City and Washington D.C. on September 11, 2001 was horrified. Everyone was injured to their human core. Everyone grappled with a mixture of fear, sadness, anger, incomprehension, and loss. Not everyone wants to go to war. Not everyone believes that revenge will secure peace, that suspended civil liberties will secure safety, that getting back to business as usual is the solution. Not everyone believes the roots of terrorism simply rest in a fanatical and irrational hatred for freedom, democracy, or the United States. This anthology is a collection of writings that gives voice to the diverse perspectives that the American people did not have an opportunity to hear despite three days of commercial-free, 24 hour-a-day news coverage on all major networks. It seeks to broaden the debate beyond what was portrayed as a monolithic call for a swift military response, for an abandonment of due process, and for an immediate reordering of national priorities. These words and ideas come from a broad cross-section of Americans: rescue workers from the World Trade Center, family members of victims, journalists, scholars, religious figures, international voices, and community advocates.

The common orientation of these essays is their attempt to find a language that evokes love, compassion and critical thought in the face of tragedy, and their recognition of this pivotal moment in human history that will either positively propel us forward or plunge us in ever-deepening despair. Beyond feel-good calls for peace, these authors provide us with first hand accounts, discussions about transforming their own grief, historical perspectives, political analyses, and alternative strategies to achieving national security. These authors present us with a choice, a way to step forward from disorder into another world.

Kofi Taha
Active Element

table of contents

introductions

View of lower Manhattan from a candlelight vigil in Jersey City, September 15, 2001
© David Katz 2001

ten years in New York has given me one thing above all others: a mental callous almost as thick and rough as the physical one 25 years of manual labor has worn into my father's hands. Occasionally, something shatters that shell. On September 11, when the first plane hit, I was getting my papers together for work and the glaze began to melt from my eyes. When the second crashed minutes later, I sat down in front of the TV and the cynical flare untensed in my nostrils. By the time the towers began to crumble, my shell had been pierced and my sarcastic mouth had no words.

What followed was two days of scrambling through busy signals, emails, unknowing, rumor, and word of mouth to make sure all in my immediate circle were safe. Then, I prepared myself for the worst in American militarism, impulsive nationalism, and anti-Muslim/anti-Palestine propaganda. After two mind-numbing weeks of essays, opinions, and critiques from the "Left" filling my inbox (I stopped watching TV a few days after September 11), I found myself at a fundraiser for CAAAV (Organizing Asian Communities), listening to Angela Davis.

My callous had repaired itself, thick as ever. Five minutes into Davis' speech (printed in this anthology), I turned to my friend and said: "Is she gonna tell me something I haven't heard or read already?" See, alternative media, dependent on the low overhead/production costs of digital distribution, had already overloaded me via email and the Internet. And Angela wasn't adding anything new; there was no blinding light emanating from her hair.

But as I settled in to listen, something changed. I began to immerse myself in the situation, sitting in a room full of friends and activists, living and breathing in a city that had just lost thousands, listening to someone speak passionately to an audience that hungrily gave its attention. By the end I was standing and clapping with everyone else, like we had just voted her in as president of the United States.

I left that night injected with passion, inspired to talk, listen, start conversations, get busy, build movement, and make change, all in one night.

I didn't hear anything breathtakingly new but what was different was the context. I was in a room full of people I felt connected to, not sitting alone in front of my computer. I was listening to someone speak passionately, not reading an email easier to delete than forward. And I communicated and debated with people in mutual respect, not letting my anger bubble quietly and cool into a hard shell.

But how exactly did that deep emotional cynicism return? What had happened during those two weeks?

I realized the dissociation I felt from 9/11 started to grow only hours after the tower collapses. Sitting in front of my TV in Brooklyn for six hours straight, the tragedy only visible through a media filter and a cloud of smoke growing darker and darker from the direction of lower Manhattan, somewhere between the wave of red, white, and blue of TV newsrooms and human tragedy stories, I began to feel detached.

Because what I wanted to hear about was the inevitable wave of hate crimes, the history of US military aggression that created the conditions for the attack, and the loss of more innocent lives abroad. I wanted to hear about the hundreds of undocumented immigrants who worked in building maintenance and food service as much as the stories of the investment bankers that they served for less than minimum wage, day in, day out. See, my mom used to mop floors and empty trash cans at an army base, and, at the very least, I wanted the media coverage to include people like me and my mom.

Watching the tragic and countless pieces on businessmen and firefighters made me immediately wonder why those stories were the focus, who was selecting them, and with what motive. My only conclusion was that they were selected in order to gain sympathy from middle white America and lead it into rage and bloodlust. The tragedy had been claimed by the media, annexed like Hawaii and Puerto Rico, "discovered" like the "New World." The national debate and discourse didn't include me because it was a monologue towards war. It was a conversation happening in another room between people without my interests in mind. Being silenced turned my sympathy into anger and callousness. I didn't care and I sank into a quiet, soft, dull spot on my couch.

It was through speaking to people in my community – political, emotional, and geographic – that pushed me out of that disempowering mute anger. It was through conversations with Jeremy, an activist and friend who lost his father on September 11th, listening to Angela Davis at the CAAAV fundraiser, and really reading some of the email analyses and opinions I received, that I discovered the necessity of opening my ears, voicing my thoughts, and creating an open space for alternative conversation, community, and action.

3

This book is a space for that dialogue, constructed by six editors with different stories, different (and even conflicting) views. Our common thread, however, is our way of feeling this tragedy and understanding it, through ways outside of the mainstream discourse, in hushed tones and words spoken in confidentiality, wary of being called insensitive and unpatriotic though it's only our way of relating, passionately and intimately. Listen...

---

a s I watched the second tower fall live on CNN, I began fearing the worst. How would Americans respond to such a horrific sight? As the days passed, CNN and all other media outlets began to bang the drum of war. Instead of presenting the plane crashes within the context of US sanctioned terror in Latin America, the Middle East, Southeast Asia, and Africa, the media outlets promoted a jingoistic one-sided view that called for a US retaliation without remorse and regret for the loss of innocent lives.

Locally, I feared for the way Latino and other immigrant communities would respond. In California, many laws and measures have been created that criminalize the Latino community. From the passage of Prop 187 (no social services for the undocumented) in 1994 to the recent passage of Prop 21 (anti-youth crime initiative) in 2000, imagery of Latino "gang-bangers" and "illegals" have fed into the racist anxieties of many older white conservative voters who fear that they are losing their power in a state that is now majority people of color. The Latino community has constantly been bombarded with the idea that they do not belong and are not American. For this reason and a lack of economic opportunities, throughout history, many Latinos have joined the armed forces to prove their patriotism and support themselves. Since the 9/11 incident Latinos have been forced once again to prove their patriotism. Like George Bush said, you either stand with the United States or with the terrorists. So under the pressure of being blamed for economic recessions, "overpopulation," social service overload, and bringing down the "standards" of public education, many Latinos have chosen to bring out the flags and let America know that we are red, white, and blue, through and through.

The stakes are now rising. The right has taken advantage of this tragedy to push through unconstitutional laws in the form of the "anti-terrorist" Patriot bill, which will be used to incriminate all those unsupportive and critical of the Bush regime: labor organizers, immigrant and civil rights activists, prison activists, education reformers, feminists, gays and lesbians, immigrants, and people of color. We are entering a new phase of McCarthyism. The Patriot bill and other measures will allow for a domestic war on social justice movements and the gutting of the little civil rights and liberties that still exist as a result of the 1960s civil rights movements.

Nobel Peace Laureate Rigoberta Menchu recently said that she neither wanted to stand with Bush (who represents US repression and violence), nor with terrorists. She advocated creating a new voice that would stand for economic, social, and global justice. Her words speak the truth. In these difficult times it is our responsibility to create that third voice of justice. A voice that defends indigenous rights in Chiapas, Guatemala, and Palestine, that demands a world where Latinos no longer have to be asked if they are "illegal" and face that inhumane gauntlet called the US/Mexico border, and that defends the civil and human rights of Muslim and Arab communities. This new voice will call for an end to the terrorism that began over 500 years ago when Columbus landed on the island of Guanahani, initiating the massacre of millions of Taino people, and continues to this day with the killing of innocent civilians in Afghanistan. We are at a critical moment in history. Let our voice define and transform the 21st century.

- Luis Sanchez

as activists, we have been asking, "What makes this bombing any different than the hundreds of thousands of Iraqi children killed by sanctions, then the innocents blown up in the Sudan and Afghanistan a couple years ago?" But it is different. This is an issue that hits us where we live and people are scared. Those people are our families, and a lot of people have alienated their families and friends over this issue. I am one of them. My relationship with several of my family members have been strained or communication has stopped out right. Part of me feels like, if you can't talk to your family about political stuff, how are you gonna talk to strangers? Part of me feels like, ahh, let it lie. But Afghani kids getting bombed in the night can't let it lie...

I come from a very pro-military family. My mom was a teacher for the military. I grew up on military bases and have first hand knowledge of what American imperialism looks like in the day to day interactions overseas. I was living on an army base during the Gulf War in Germany. I was 10 years old. There was no questioning allowed, no discussion of our actions in the engagement. There was just right or wrong and we were right. They gave us dog tags of every soldier. I actually baked cookies and wrote letters to my soldier. Many of the kids I grew up with either become anti-military or pro-military, because they have to have some way to explain it to themselves. Right now we are seeing that all across this country, people grasping for an answer to explain this, and the media and government are all too willing to point fingers.

5

Another concern with this current situation is the "Left's" response. It's already painfully apparent that the peace movement is building off a lot of the momentum of the anti-globalization movement, which didn't frame that struggle to include folks of color, the people at the center of this conflict and globalization. Who do sweatshops effect? People of color. Who are the last hired and first fired here when they ship the jobs overseas? People of color. Without a strong anti-racist analysis, the anti-globalization movement sounds frighteningly close to ultra nationalist, right wing rhetoric, and without actually listening to Middle Eastern/South Asian people, the ones intimately affected by recent events, it will just be white people telling people of color how to think all over again.

It's really important the way we go about discussing these issues. Too many people are buying into the mass hysteria and fear that is circulating in this country. The subtitle of this book, "Conversations in a Time of Terror" is American-centric and feeds that hysteria by emphasizing the word "terror." It's been a time of terror for folks of color, in and out of this country, for centuries. So to designate this as a time of terror makes American fear (and really, white privileged fear) the focus of analysis, rather than the aftermath of 9/11 that is rippling around the world. I know we are trying to reach a broad spectrum of folks, but it's necessary to understand that it is Third World people who have been bearing the brunt of US terrorist attacks since this country's inception. And it is those in Afghanistan, in Palestine, in all of the Middle East, in American ghettoes, in radical organizations, who will bear the brunt of the repercussions of 9/11.

- Walidah Imarisha

during the first week after the tragedy, the Left played host to a series of meetings that many left from feeling disillusioned and lost. They were sectarian and process heavy. I didn't go to a single one. It wasn't where I was at. I was grieving and despondent and lamenting humanity's pain. I wanted to examine every face on the posters at Union Square and make it real. I wanted to surround myself with my cadre of dear friends, sharing meals and holding hands. I needed to "go in." And I did that upstate, pulling weeds out of the earth and feeling the sun on my shoulders. I started to trip on "meaning." My conception of the world, of right and wrong and the way things ought to be was turned on its head, calling into question my sense of purpose. There are times in life when you do some heavy growing and I was feeling the growing pains. After a furious four-day thinking binge, I awoke with a sense of peace.

And when the dust settled, it came time to "go out." To get mad and feel hope. After the disaster, I got involved a few projects. I've begun volunteering with the Salvation Army, doing casework for family members who lost loved ones and folks who lost their jobs. We write vouchers to cover phone bills, utilities, rent, food. I've also been helping the Arab American Family Support Center in Brooklyn set up a volunteer coordination program and I'm working with a collective of artists and activists to organize an International Gathering of Hope (www.gatheringofhope.org). It's a commemoration of the victims of the World Trade Center and Pentagon attacks but also of the victims of violence across the globe.

People have criticized my generation for being apathetic. I don't think that's the case. We grew up with a false sense of security. Blinders on in the belly of the beast. We'd begun to change that: challenging the Coke vs. Pepsi electoral races of recent years, the geography of nowhere that Walmart and Home Depot's colonial expansion cultivates, Nike's slave labor, prisons as the fastest growing public housing sector, and agitating to excommunicate the unholy trinity of the IMF, World Bank, and WTO.

I grew up thinking that history was something that happened in the past, moved by a few uber-humans we pedestalize and can't relate to. But it wasn't a cosmically inspired alignment of right time, right place, and super leaders that won Blacks the vote or workers a minimum wage. It was a lot of long, hard work by people like you and me. Lots of us. People of conscience who refuse to sit back in the face of injustices.

So I'm calling all Jedi knights, all history-shapers. The yin yang balance of the universe has been thrown out of whack. We gotta push the pendulum back or we'll vault off into darkness, into a world where the gap between rich and poor grows to a chasm, where dissent is suppressed, where political and economic violence reign. We can't let the moral majority and Washington "consensus" proscribe their vacuous vision for a homogenized and sickly planet. We need to get off our booties and find a way to do something that makes sense for each of us. We need to take risks; we got a lot of building to do. Another world IS possible. Now, more than ever, is the time to offer up an alternate vision. Let's insert ourselves into history.

7

- Beka Economopoulos

On September 11th I was in a trendy café in Durban, South Africa, after attending the World Conference Against Racism. My friend and I quickly became the center of attention as everyone wanted to know if these two Americans were from New York City, if they know people there, and how they felt about the country collapsing before their eyes. Like every other person from the Middle East I repeated in my head: "Please, let it be one of their own, please don't let the terrorists look like me." I knew that though McVeigh and Kaczinksy didn't make all white people potential terrorists, these handful of hijackers would instantly confirm the hundreds of millions of people of the Middle East as inherently violent, more suspect than ever before.

I returned to the United States almost a month after the attacks to intense war hysteria and a political climate that endorsed attacks on Middle Easterners and Muslims, or people who looked like them. There were stories of "mistaken" identities: Sikh Indians being mistakenly targeted for Muslims, Mexicans for Arabs. And increasingly, since the attacks, there has been a surge in a desire to understand the "Other." What is Islam? Who is Osama bin Laden? As if these attacks and a strategy to avoid future ones could be explained in a passage from the Qu'ran or in some aspect of bin Laden's personality at age 12.

In her article "The Algebra of Infinite Justice," Arundhati Roy explains that terrorism is a symptom of a larger problem, not the problem itself. What is missing in news reports and patriotic proclamations by government representatives is a historical and political context in which to place these latest symptoms. So I have to ask, in a historical context, what does the subtitle of this book, "Conversations in a Time of Terror," really mean? Certainly with 25 million infected with HIV, Africa knows the meaning of terror, especially as American pharmaceutical companies refuse to sell AIDS treatment drugs at rates affordable for the majority of Africans infected, which is particularly devastating for pregnant women with HIV. Certainly Iraqi women and children know the meaning terror, having been deprived of food and medicines for the last decade due to US imposed sanctions meant to destabilize Saddam Hussein. Meanwhile, the sanctions have resulted in 1.5 million Iraqis dead while President Hussein gains popular support.

It's not hard to see why some in the world hate the United States. The sickness underlying the symptoms in this case is US foreign policy, not an unconditional and irrational hate of freedom and democracy, as media and politicians have claimed. It has been a time of terror for many people in the world for a very long time and America has only taken notice now because Americans have become victims too. It is our task to re-evaluate US policies and actions throughout the world. It is time to be outraged that the United States can pull out of an international conference against racism and that this country is bombing an already devastated Afghani people. It is time to engage with the rest of the world on what it means to live in terror and what it means to be free.

- Shaffy Moeel

One of the hardest parts of the grieving process for me, losing my father in Tower I of the WTC on September 11, 2001, is the complete collapse of public/private. The vocabulary of mourning gets radically re-invented when the machinations of American imperialism take the life of a loved one. Usually, when a person loses a parent you fall out of the fold for a while, some close friends and family hold you down, perhaps some colleagues send their sympathy, and you gradually re-enter the complexities of as Gil Scott Heron has phrased the "everyday." Your family's pain does not become part in parcel of a national and international dialogue, spiteful ruling class politicians don't send you "letters of sympathy," American flags don't become the commonplace symbol in a language of trauma, 500 people (most of whom you do not know) don't show up to your dad's memorial service. To add to the dread and confusion in our house on September 11, I share the name of the man who heroically resisted his captors in the plane over PA. And so, while negotiating the horror of not knowing my dad's whereabouts, our family entertained countless emails and calls from concerned colleagues, comrades, and friends anxious about my own safety. Ruling class politicians, "in the name of the father, the victims, and the victim's families," perform hollow pronouncements of empathy for you and your loved ones to rationalize immanent slaughter and devastation. Blame is an expected stage in the grieving process. As an anti-imperialist, I immediately turned to history to make sense of my dad's death. I was comforted by Fredric Jameson, writing in the London Review of Books:

Historical events, however, are not punctual, but extend in a before and after of time which only gradually reveal themselves. It has, to be sure, been pointed out that the Americans created bin Laden during the Cold War (and in particular the Soviet war in Afghanistan) and that this is therefore a textbook example of dialectical reversal. But the seeds of the event are buried deeper than that. They are to be found wholesale massacres of the Left systematically encouraged and directed by the Americans in an earlier period.

9

I realize more and more how much of my relationship with my father constantly challenged that same public/private line. The "seeds" of my own activism are found in the stances, positions, and actions of my parents. My father and I practiced the endless art of debate and argument pertaining to questions of the political. I learned about Woody Guthrie, Jazz, and the Blues through my dad, and carried that into a profound love for Hip Hop. My dad first pulled my coats to Marxism, the Black Panthers (the first books I stole from my folk's awesome basement library), Richard Wright, and detective fiction. I was often mad or disappointed in what I perceived as a mellowing out (or selling out) of my dad's once more radically pronounced views. It took listening to his eulogies to really get some clarity on how much my dad's sacrifices enabled my own radical activism. The endless drudge of going to work, to provide, and enable my actions was my father's sacrifice. A sacrifice that this system never acknowledged or paid him what he's worth, and ultimately, thanked him for by violently ripping him from his family.

- **Jeremy M. Glick**

This is an unconventional anthology, in a number of ways. First, the two titles are meant to enable it to enter into multiple spaces, engage as many circles as possible to provoke more dialogue. Though promoting conversation doesn't sound extremely ambitious, in this atmosphere of dissent-killing fear, it is a huge first step forward. This anthology is not only a space for debate and dialogue, it is an opportunity to emerge out of the chaos and disorder of 9/11 and build another world. The editors are united in the belief that the policies of the US, the New World Order, is actually a disorder stemming from the mental illnesses of men in power, and that another world is not only possible, but necessary in these times of terror and uncertainty.

For readers, this anthology isn't supposed to be picked at like a buffet, with only certain articles read. There is a progression and it is meant to be consumed whole: skin, uncooked parts, and all. This anthology has been constructed more fluidly, like a conversation, with thoughts and themes that recur and ideas that are started in one place and picked up at another, all in the hope that it is read in its entirety. Some parts are sweet and easy on the palate while others are bitter and uncomfortable – please chew attentively on everything.

There are things in this anthology you won't like. There are things I don't like. There's a significant amount of humor, which many will accuse of being inappropriate, while others will point to the effectiveness of using it to voice dissent. Some will laugh, some will be offended, some confused, some angry, some elated, some relieved, some I can't predict. But as long as it's something, not indifference. As long as it empowers us to talk, listen, and debate. Where the conversations go from there, into collective movement and action, or into a quiet, soft, dull spot on a couch, that's for each of us to determine.

For my part, I wanna spread the word, get passionate, think of solutions, strategize, get busy, build movements, and make change, all in one night, or at least in our lifetimes.

- Jee Kim

NOT IN MY NAME

"I thought the name The Twin Towers was curious. The name made them sound like children, like they were rather defenseless."

- Elsa Mora, Artist

8:45 AM, SEPTEMBER 11TH
Usman Farman

My name is Usman Farman and I graduated from Bentley with a Finance degree last May. I am 21 years old, turning 22 in October; I am Pakistani and I am Muslim. Until September 10th 2001, I used to work at the World Trade Center in building 7. I had friends and acquaintances who worked in Tower 1 right across from me. Some made it out, and some are still unaccounted for. I survived this horrible event. I'd like to share with you what I went through that awful day, with the hopes that we can all stay strong together through this tragedy of yet untold proportions. As I found out, regardless of who we are and where we come from, we only have each other.

I commute into the city every morning on the train from New Jersey. Rather, I used to. I still can't believe what is happening. That morning I woke up and crawled out of bed. I was thinking about flaking on the train and catching the late one, I remember telling myself that I just had to get to work on time. I ended up catching the 7:48 train which put me in Hoboken at 8:20. When I got there I thought about getting something to eat, I decided against it and took the PATH train to the World Trade Center. I arrived at the World Trade at 8:40. I walked into the lobby of building 7 at 8:45, that's when the first plane hit. Had I taken the late train or gotten a bite to eat, I would have been 5 minutes late and walking over the crosswalk. Had that happened, I would have been caught under a rain of fire and debris, I wouldn't be here talking to you. I'd be dead.

I was in the lobby and I heard the first explosion; it didn't register. They were doing construction outside and I thought some scaffolding had fallen. I took the elevators up to my office on the 27th floor. When I walked in, the whole place was empty. There were no alarms, no sprinklers, nothing. Our offices are, or rather, were on the south side of building 7. We were close enough to the North and South Towers that I could literally throw a stone from my window and hit the North tower with it. My phone rang and I spoke with my mother. As I was telling her that I was leaving, I saw an explosion rip out of the second building. I called my friend in Boston, waking her up and telling her to tell everyone I'm okay and that I was leaving. I looked down one last time and saw the square and fountain that I eat lunch in was covered in smoldering debris. Apparently, I was one of the last to leave my building; when I was on the way up in the elevators, my co-workers from the office were in the stairwells coming down. When I evacuated, there was no panic. People were calm and helping each other; a pregnant woman was being carried down the stairwell. I'll spare the more gruesome details of what I saw- those are things that no one should ever have to see and beyond human decency to describe. Those are things which will haunt me for the rest of my life. My heart goes out to everyone who lost their lives that day and those who survived with the painful reminders of what once was. Acquaintances of mine who made it out of the towers only got out because a thousand people formed a human chain to find their way out of the smoke.

Everyone was a hero that day. We were evacuated to the north side of building 7. The security people told us to go north and not to look back. Five city blocks later I stopped and turned around to watch. With a thousand people staring, we saw in shock as the first tower collapsed. No one could believe it was happening, it is still all too-surreal to imagine. The next thing I remember is that a dark cloud of glass and debris about 50 stories high came tumbling towards us. I turned around and ran as fast as possible. I didn't realize until yesterday that the reason I'm still feeling so sore was that I fell down trying to get away. What happened next is why I'm writing this.

I was on my back, facing this massive cloud that was approaching It must have been 600 feet off but everything was already dark. I normally wear a pendant around my neck, inscribed with an Arabic prayer for safety, similar to the cross. A Hasidic Jewish man came up to me and held the pendant in his hand. He read the Arabic out loud for a second. What he said next, I will never forget. With a deep Brooklyn accent he said "Brother, if you don't mind, there is a cloud of glass coming at us. Grab my hand, let's get the hell out of here." He helped me stand up and we ran for what seemed like forever without looking back. He was the last person I would ever have thought to help me. If it weren't for him I probably would have been engulfed in shattered glass and debris. I finally stopped about 20 blocks away and looked in horror as tower 2 came crashing down. Fear came over me as I realized that some people were evacuated to the streets below the towers. Like I said before, no one could have thought those buildings could collapse. We turned around and in shock and disbelief and began the trek to midtown. It took me three hours to get to my sister's office at 3rd Ave and 47th St. Some streets were completely deserted, completely quiet, no cars, no nothing. Just the distant wail of sirens. I managed to call home and say I was okay and get in touch with co-workers and friends whom I feared were lost. We managed to get a ride to New Jersey. Looking back, as I crossed the George Washington Bridge, I could not see the towers. It had really happened. As the world continues to reel from this tragedy, people in the streets are lashing out. Not far from my home, a Pakistani woman was run over on purpose as she was crossing the parking lot to put groceries in her car. Her only fault? That she had her head covered and was wearing the traditional clothing of my homeland. I am afraid for my family's well being within our community. My older sister is too scared to take the subway into work now. My 8 year old sister's school is under lockdown and armed watch by police.

13

Violence only begets violence, and by lashing out at each other in fear and hatred, we will become no better than the faceless cowards who committed this atrocity. If it weren't for that man who helped me get up, I would most likely be in the hospital right now, if not dead. Help came from the least expected place and only goes to show that we are all in this together, regardless of race, religion, or ethnicity. Those are principles that this country was founded on. Friends or strangers, in a time of crisis, you would want the nearest person to help you if you needed it. My help came from a man who I would never have thought would normally even speak to me.

My name is Usman Farman and I graduated from Bentley with a Finance degree last May. I am 21 years old, turning 22 in October; I am Pakistani and I am Muslim, and I too have been victimized by this awful tragedy. The next time you feel angry about this and perhaps want to retaliate in your own way, please remember these words: "Brother, if you don't mind, there is a cloud of glass coming at us. Grab my hand, let's get the hell out of here."

From: Kym Clark
To: Jee Kim
Subject: Jeremy Glick, FYI

Daily News reports Jeremy Glick as having been a passenger on one of the flights...

Jeremy, as I understand it, is an activist also in the poetry scene, perhaps out of Jersey. I hear his name so much that when I heard that I just threw it out there, thinking folks that know him might be able to drop him or his family a line to see if he was really on there.

Just trying to pass on info.

GROUND ZERO
James Creedon, NYC paramedic and student activist at The City University of New York.

Hello all. Thank you very much for the many many notes of support and condolence. Things are very difficult here in New York City, and I'm just trying to keep on top of things. I thought Iwould share a bit about what happened to me on September 11th, 2001 to answer questions and let you know a little bit more about the events here...

I woke up Tuesday morning to the radio and heard that a building had been struck by an airplane. I honestly thought it was a historical piece about the B-52 bomber that hit the Empire State Building back in the 1940s... Once I knew the real deal, that two planes had struck, I put my uniform on and headed off to my station.

From where I was standing, it was about half a block to World Trade Center 1 (North Tower). I could see flames and smoke billowing out of the building and debris was landing all around me. There were body parts scattered on the ground and it was pretty clear how bad things were...

Moments later, I heard an enormous roar and felt the ground shaking. I looked up to the tower and saw what looked like an umbrella being opened up–like a starburst at the fireworks. I was directly underneath it and I could see girders shooting out from the building. I immediately began to run southwest, towards a building that had some sort of opening. I already felt rocks landing on my back and helmet and there were girders falling right near me. I made it perhaps 30 feet before being knocked off my feet. I went about ten feet through the air and landed rolling on a set of steps. My helmet was gone, my phone, my stethoscope...

15

This was the scariest moment of my life. The air was black with ash and debris and I literally couldn't see a thing. People were screaming and some were clearly seriously injured. We couldn't breathe and our mouths eyes and noses watered and burned... I stayed crouching on the ground, covering my head and

© Richard Yeh 2001

"The silence is amazing. The quiet of people who have just had the wind blown out of them. Speechlessness. A silent New York. "
- Kiini Ibura Salaam

breathing through my shirt. A few minutes later, the smoke began to clear and I was able to make out a few other figures. We held on to each other and were able to make it to a restaurant where we started gathering water for eye flushes. Ambulances and fire trucks were overturned, walkways were collapsed, and people were running and screaming.

After a half-hour of giving out water, I started to help out with moving other people to the waterfront where we were loading them onto boats and ferries. But soon we had to clear out from there also because the second tower was coming down. I was holding a 3-year-old girl at the time and we lost sight of her mother. We all ran as hard as we could, while trying to carry as many people as possible. There were many injuries and many more people with smoke inhalation or blindness.

Eventually, we regrouped on a pier farther southeast and got more people loaded up to bring them to New Jersey. I helped here for a while and ended up taking one of the last boats to NJ to help with triage and treatment there, by order of my supervisor.

An hour or two later, I was redeployed to Manhattan, then taken to the hospital to be treated for injuries. Luckily, I got off well. I have a sprained ankle, twisted knee, miscellaneous burns and abrasions, and had to have glass and gravel removed from my arms and back. That night I stayed in the hospital on semi-active duty and this morning (Wednesday) I worked a 911 shift uptown and then went down to Ground Zero to assist with rescue efforts.

Overall, I feel very lucky. Many of us thought there would be chemical/biological agents in the explosion but thus far we are in the clear. I have made it out in one piece but the same cannot be said for many others.

Especially sad and difficult to me is the loss of two members of my own team. They were killed in collapse of World Trade Center 2 (South Tower), along with hundreds of other rescuers.

Tonight, I want to thank all of you for your calls and emails. I feel honored to have been in your thoughts and prayers and am unspeakably grateful for each and every friendship that has revealed itself. But more importantly, I ask that you keep the in your thoughts the lives and sacrifices of the many rescue workers. I have lost friends, and I can honestly say that they were some of the most caring, deeply committed, and selfless people I have ever met.

Finally, I want to urge all of us to remember the complexities of the world we live in. This is a tragic act, one that has destroyed or forever altered the lives of countless people. It is also an act that occurs in particular context, one in which the United States is guilty of this exact same kind of crime, only on a greater and more gruesome scale. Let us take from this the inspiration to create a world free from imperialism in all its manifestations, one that moves us from the civil war that is capitalism to a higher form of society.

With love and rage,
James Creedon

© Richard Yeh 2001

17

FIRST WRITING SINCE
Suheir Hammad

1. there have been no words.

i have not written one word.

no poetry in the ashes south of canal street.

no prose in the refrigerated trucks driving debris and dna.

not one word.

today is a week, and seven is of heavens, gods, science.

evident out my kitchen window is an abstract reality.

sky where once was steel.

smoke where once was flesh.

fire in the city air and i feared for my sister's life in a way never

before. and then, and now, i fear for the rest of us.

first, please god, let it be a mistake, the pilot's heart failed, the

plane's engine died.

then please god, let it be a nightmare, wake me now.

please god, after the second plane, please, don't let it be anyone

who looks like my brothers.

i do not know how bad a life has to break in order to kill.

i have never been so hungry that i willed hunger

i have never been so angry as to want to control a gun over a pen.

not really.

even as a woman, as a palestinian, as a broken human being.

never this broken.

18

more than ever, i believe there is no difference.

the most privileged nation, most americans do not know the difference

between indians, afghanis, syrians, muslims, sikhs, hindus.

more than ever, there is no difference.

```
From: Jee Kim
To: Kym Clark
Subject: shit...

kym, is this confirmed??? i knew/know jeremy, he was/is
good friends with darryl. please let me know if you hear
anything.
```

BROOKLYN DIARY
Kenny Bruno, CorpWatch
September 19, 2001

Day 1

When this happens, you want to be with your children. My son seems so
unreachable, though just a few miles away, across the East River in Manhattan.
When the second tower blows, I try to get to him by bicycle but can't get
through the smoke or the police lines. In the evening I'm able to get to himand
we walk back home over the Brooklyn Bridge. It is a perversely, stubbornly
beautiful sunset, with a orange sky behind the Statue of Liberty and light
reflecting off the buildings, such as I have seen many times from that bridge.

The Empire State, the Chrysler, the CitiCorp building, all the midtown skyscrapers look, as usual, like parts of the Emerald City. People are taking photographs. Everyone is calm. Behind us, where the twin towers used to be, is only black smoke.

It had really happened.

Skyscrapers were never my favorite part of New York, nor, for me at least, an important symbol. I prefer the boardwalk of Coney Island, the restaurants of Chinatown, the galleries and lofts of Soho, the brownstones of Harlem and Brooklyn, Central Park, Madison Square Garden. When I used to commute by bicycle into Manhattan over the bridge, I stared at the towers but I never loved them. I thought about the conglomerations of corporate and financial power inside. I thought and re-thought my role as a tiny part of a movement that aimed to chip away at that power, non-violently, through coalitions, through information, through persuasion, through intelligence, through resistance. I never dreamed the buildings could actually disintegrate, in a matter of seconds.

19

```
From: Kym Clark
To: Jee Kim
Subject: what I know

Ibrahim saw Jeremy's name in the Daily News. Not
confirmed that he boarded.
```

In the morning I partially broke a pledge, made after the December Supreme Court decision selecting George Bush as president, never to watch a speech of his on TV. I started to watch his address to the nation, but I could only stand a few minutes before switching to radio. Alas, Bush was himself - shallow, emotionally disconnected, mostly concerned with getting through his remarks on message. At a time like this, it's especially painful to have a nincompoop as a president.

Evil begets goodness. This was the epitome of evil: deliberate mass murder of innocent people. And yet everywhere in this city famous for its gruffness, people were being good to each other. Free food, water, shoes, rides, hugs, nods of understanding.

By the end of the day I know that my family has been lucky. We are all safe, none of our relatives or friends was in the building. But like many or most New Yorkers, we are just one or two degrees of separation from the tragedy. The father of a boy in my daughter's 4th grade class called his wife, the head of the

PTA, from the 101st floor when the first plane hit to say goodbye. He hasn't been heard from since. Another neighbor, a man I saw on Saturdays during the youth soccer season or when picking my daughter up from a playdate, made it out of the building with his wife. He told her to go get the kids and then he went back in to try to help. He hasn't come back out.

Day 2
We are the Dr. Frankenstein of nations, creating terrorist monsters we then have to kill off. Bush says we won't distinguish between terrorists and those that harbor them. A letter writer to the *Times* says we must fight those "who hate our values." Well, many French people hate our values. Many religious people hate our values. I often hate our values (not freedom and democracy, but commercialism and materialism).

© David Katz 2001

It is so hard to see "our values" as others see them, through our actions as a nation. Most of us never even try. So we are in a dangerous situation. Because if you combine the idea that we are at war with the idea that any friend of our enemy is our enemy and then consider anyone who hates our values to be our enemy and define our values as "freedom," you can justify killing so many millions.

Day 3
Tired of seeing the plane crash into the tower over and over in my dreams, I bring this new danger into my home early in the form of the *New York Post*, which practically screams for blood. "THE FACE OF HATE" reads the caption

under a photo of an Arab suspect. "The heavens need to fall on their heads...they need to bleed...now...Who are they? Who cares?...Bombs Away." No wonder the Yemeni man who sells me the newspaper every day is frightened. No wonder the police have practically locked down the Arab neighborhood around Atlantic Avenue. No wonder none of the Muslim kids showed up to school today. Even George Bush, in a staged phone call to Mayor Giuliani and Governor Pataki, has called for tolerance for Arab-Americans, albeit in his stumbling, scripted, unconvincing way. In Bay Ridge, Arab Americans are beat up, cursed at. There are rumors in the Arab community of killings in Clinton Hill, though I can't find any reporting of it at all. We are far, very far, from the tolerance necessary to avoid more bloodshed of innocents. The *Times* quotes an Afghan man selling fertilizer in a market, saying that though the terrorists are "enemies of God," nevertheless "Americans should look into their hearts and minds about why someone would kill themselves and others." Senator Chuck Schumer and most of our leaders are quite confident they already know why. "They hate our freedom," says the liberal Democrat from New York. We are far, very far, from being able to look at ourselves, our role. That is understandable at this time. But our "leaders" are taking us farther away.

21

All disagreement with the US will be suspect as sympathetic to terrorism. It will be a bad time for dissent of any kind. Today shock is partly subsiding, replaced by grief. We begin assuming the missing are dead. The local news indulges in grief pornography, repeatedly showing sobbing relatives holding up photographs of the missing. Passing the fire station, a burly firefighter back from a 30-hour shift bursts into ear-shattering sobs on the shoulder of a colleague, the two remain in an embrace until after I've gone. The Union Street firehouse in Brooklyn has lost 12 of its 30 fire fighters, probably some of the ones who came and opened up the hydrant as a sprinkler for our block party last weekend. Their sidewalk is a memorial of flowers and candles. There are announcements in many neighborhoods of counseling for kids, a vigil and march for victims, a clothing, food and money drive for families.

The American flags come out on cars, on the street, on the front page of the bloodthirsty *New York Post*. We who have been lucky are tempted to think things are going back to normal. But then we remember, it cannot go back to normal for Kelly, or Nicole, or Liz Anne, or their kids, or thousands and thousands who have had a father or child erased from their lives as the towers were erased from the skyline.

Day 4

I walk back uptown but when I get to the edge of the "frozen zone," there are people desperately trying to deliver supplies to the Red Cross who cannot enter the area. So I deliver bags for them, walking back and forth from Canal St. to Chambers for a few hours carrying bags of hard hats, boots, batteries and clothing. Bush arrives and it gets tense downtown. Fighter jets are circling through the clouds above. Military police have taken control of the streets, shouting at NYC cops, firefighters, and rescue workers to get on the sidewalk. Our local heroes are not too happy about suddenly being bossed around and some are grumbling that they just want to get back to work and this presidential visit is getting in their way. Others say it's about time he showed up.

On the way home I meet a friend who tells the story of a Bangladeshi colleague, a Muslim woman who wears a head scarf, who was punched in the face yesterday and told "It's your fault, it's your fault." Evil begets goodness, but it also begets more evil. The very essence of the evil act, the targeting of innocent people because they are vaguely associated with an "enemy," is being repeated on the streets.

At the fire station a few blocks away the crowd chants "USA, USA," and sings "Amazing Grace." A small group then sings "Down By The Riverside." Not everyone seems to think it's the right song for the moment but no one shouts them down. This is not the time for arguing amongst ourselves; it's a time for togetherness. The fire fighters, still exhausted and in mourning, are visibly moved by the outpouring of love and respect.

I am proud of my neighborhood – its generosity, strength, solidarity, resilience, compassion, and tolerance, its support for its heroes. A moment after I walk in the door, there is a ruckus outside. Two women shout for us to call the precinct. There's a roaming group of teenagers on the block, loud, drunk and confrontational, and they have spray-painted "Fuck Arabs" on the sidewalk. My neighbor has some spray paint remover, and we try to scrub the sidewalk clean.

SEPTEMBER 1, 1939
W. H. Auden

I sit in one of the dives

On Fifty-second Street

Uncertain and afraid

As the clever hopes expire

Of a low dishonest decade:

Waves of anger and fear

Circulate over the bright

And darkened lands of the earth,

Obsessing our private lives;

The unmentionable odour of death

Offends the September night.

AN AMERICAN IN PALESTINE
Elizabeth Price

As a Bay Area resident living in the West Bank, the news of the terrorist attack in America has destroyed me twice over. I was working at my American development organization when we heard the news of the first plane. We crowded around the TV to watch what we thought was a local air disaster, only to realize, as the second plane impacted, that something was terribly wrong. I spent the next ten hours glued to the TV with my Palestinian co-workers and in-laws, stunned and grief-stricken as we watched the indescribable human tragedy unfold. Taking breaks only to call my family about my brother who lives in NY and talk to friends who work near the WTC, I watched as my world crumbled around me. Even though I live in a place where military bombing is a daily occurrence, sounds of engines in the sky strike fear into my heart, and Palestinian death toll grows daily, I was totally unprepared the scenes of carnage and loss on CNN. Even though I have lived through war in the last ten months, I feel like I only lost my innocence on Tuesday, September 11.

I feel like I have been forced into the cold, harsh world of adulthood, where memories sear and hiding places are lost. I am used to telling my parents, as Israeli tank shells fall nearby, that my life is safe and everything is ok. But now, it is them that I worry for. The loss of innocence of the American people is a terrible thing and the scale of loss is a trauma that I wish history did not have to record as fact. Every morning since that day, I wake up in dread, growing into the knowledge that evil has crept in this world for good. That was the first destruction, and again, I am lucky that I am scarred only indirectly. I cannot imagine the horrors that have visited countless families in America whose lives were destroyed more than I can even imagine.

© Lina Palotta 2001

The second destruction came when I heard of images of Palestinians celebrating being shown repeatedly in America. As the American wife of a Palestinian, I felt like I had been punched in the stomach. How could anyone celebrate this tragedy against my fellow countrymen? Here I was suffering with them from the military sieges, the bombings, and the economic misery, and they celebrate my nation's loss? Then I saw the images: eight people in one neighborhood of Jerusalem - A woman ululating, two or three boys jumping around and two men honking their horns in broad daylight and a crowd in a Lebanese camp shot guns. And I was angry. How dare they celebrate? And I was confused. Why were they celebrating when, everywhere else in the West Bank and Gaza streets, streets were empty and people sat, speechless in front of their TVs. After going to buy CNN-marathon supplies on September 11, my sister-in-law said that, in every shop, Palestinians were crowded, stunned, in front of their TVs, hoping endlessly that the rumors of Japanese Red Army involvement were true because they could not believe a Middle Eastern party would do such a thing. My father-in-law called with condolences, saying that the celebrating people had been paid money to act in front of the TV cameras. This is difficult to believe, but it is indicative of the anger and bewilderment shown by Palestinians over this image and the desire to deny all connection to these unacceptable sentiments. As these two images were shown over and over again throughout the world, I felt like I had nothing to which to cling. My birth nation under attack and my husband's nation discredited, when all were actually united in mourning and suspense.

As my Palestinian co-workers and I spent the entire of September 12 watching live coverage, the drone of Israeli Apache helicopters and F16s filled the skies and the news of 11 deaths including a little girl trickled in from a northern Palestinian town. When a CNN commentator said that the noise of planes scared him now, one colleague said she knew exactly what he meant. Now, I want to reach out to my fellow Americans and tell them that no one here is celebrating. Those images were taken in one small street in Jerusalem, before the full story was revealed and before the world found out that America had suffered a terrible tragedy. Palestinians are angry that those people dared to put the terrible events of NY and DC in the context of this region. Although American support to Israel severely depresses the Palestinian people, no one here would wish the misery of loss and death on another nation, particularly on such a scale. And I'm angry at the media organizations that played those two images over and over again for effect, making Americans think that it represented the Palestinian attitude. At best, I counted 30 people in the total footage. Compared to over three million Palestinians, that is a negligible minority but the TV stations saw a good visual story.

For a few seconds of interesting filler, those stations have destroyed the reputation of an entire people and fanned the flames of anti-Muslim and anti-Arab feelings that have already led to vandalism and violent threats on American citizens. Every day, I hear of Palestinians and Muslims who are desperate to find out if they had relatives in the WTC. I know of a Palestinian family friend in NY who ran through the debris-laded streets to find his little sister who works in Building 7 and of a close Muslim friend who spent hours on the phone trying to locate her aunt who worked on a high-numbered floor. I know that many Pakistani and Arab Muslims work in the financial institutes whose floors disappeared completely. I know that everyone everywhere is suffering together. As I grieve for my country's loss, far from my family and far from my nation, allow me to tell my fellow citizens that I am not alone in my sorrows here. The only emotions I have seen in the last few days in the Palestinian territories are unspeakable grief and the agonizing awareness that the world has lost its innocence.

25

```
To: Darryl Scipio
From: Jee Kim
Subject: FW: jeremy glick -FYI

darryl, do you know if this is true?
i pray it isn't...

jee
```

WHAT HAS CHANGED FOR ALL OF US
Barbara Kingsolver

This is what has changed for us: not what we know, but how we feel. We have always lived in a world of constant sorrow and calamity, but most of us never had to say before: It could have been me. My daughter and me on that plane, my husband in the building. I have stepped on that very pavement, I have probably sat on one of those planes. This was us, Americans at work, on vacation, going home, or just walking from one building to another. Alive, then dead. It's probably only human to admit that a stranger's death is more shattering when we can imagine it as our own. Worse disasters have happened - if ''worse'' is measured by numbers of dead - to practically every other country on earth. In my lifetime I've argued against genocide, joined campaigns for disaster aid, sent seeds to places of famine. I have mourned my fellow humans every way I've known how, but never before have their specific deaths so persistently entered my dreams. This time I am not just sad, I am in some way lost. I need to see the rest of the movie, to finish this out so the awful loop in my head might finally end.

SIXTEEN YEARS LATER
Kathleen Pequeo, Western Prison Project

Flyers of the missing at the New York Armory
© David Katz 2001

Early Tuesday morning, a dear friend called me to tell me about what had just happened in New York and Washington DC. She wanted to make sure that I heard it from someone close to me before I heard it on the radio, and with good reason. My brother was Edward Pimental, one of three Americans killed in a terrorist attack on the US Rhein-Mein Airbase in Germany in 1985. So these events affect me differently than they do most people. You cannot fathom how differently. And you don't want to know. I never imagined a day would come when tens of thousands of Americans would join my family in the awful experience of losing a family member to terrorism. For those of you who didn't lose someone close to you in this weeks events, your feelings of outrage, sorrow and anger pale in comparison to that of family members. Ten or fifteen years from now, you will have some recollection of this incident, but your distance will protect you. Family members will still be dreaming of their lost loved ones, counting their lost birthdays, weeping when new acts of terrorism are committed, and trying to put it behind them because so many others have. You think that America will never forget, but sadly, some greater act of violence will soon eclipse this and this event will, for many, fade into memory. It is the nature of violence that each act builds upon the preceding unthinkable act, making it impossible to keep track.

For the last 16 years, I have lived with the effects of terrorism and its effects. My heart goes out to the families and the support they will need for many years to come. Murder in any form is excruciating, but terrorism is different than other forms of murder because it is based in political reality. It does not happen, as some would have us believe, out of the blue. It is part of a series of horrific events that many of us are oblivious to until terrorists hurt us badly enough that we have to pay attention. Because I was struggling to understand what had happened, I found myself in the uncomfortable position of finding out more about the beliefs of the people who killed my brother. And my response to his murder has been shaped by what I have learned. Now, if I have been able to stop and listen to the beliefs of terrorists, so can you. And when you pay attention, this is what you will hear: The US has committed acts of barbarous violence against innocent civilians and must be punished. The US is made up of people willing to kill and die to destroy our way of life. We have no choice but to kill them before they kill us. Sound familiar? When Americans say this, we are in fact repeating the words of the terrorists, and that is why you will not hear them come out of my mouth.

27

CRITICAL MASS FOR FIREFIGHTERS
Georgina Silby

We had a Critical Mass bike ride the last Friday of September. It started at Union Square. This one the theme was peace and solidarity with the Fire Department, the Fire People, mostly men. So the critical mass weaved in an out of all the Fire Stations below Union Square that lost people in the collapse of the buildings. It was amazing. It was really amazing.

There were probably 500 cyclists and we were cycling down the street, chanting about peace or whatever. And then it would be quiet and we would slow down and we'd come to the most beautiful part of the street with all the candles and flowers spilling out. And the people at the front of the ride would let the fire people know what the ride was about. Everyone would cheer. At the back of the ride it would be quiet and then everyone would cheer and we would slow down, and you would know we must be going past a fire station and greeting the fire people and their altars. It was so touching, the exchange. Because you'd have this mob of cyclists, who don't normally have much in common with fire fighters and here was deep respect, from us towards them as we offered some compassion and appreciation, and from them to us since we showed up to bear witness to their suffering.

There was this sense of connection that we never felt before. And they said hey, thank you. We needed cheering up. This girl who was on roller blades, she brought some kind of prayer object. And they would kind of all come out. They were so amazed. All of the sudden, there are 500 cyclists telling them they are so brave and they appreciate them. It was so magical with the bikes; the feeling got stronger and stronger as we went. I was all the way at the end of the ride and I would just stop and talk to the firemen and you could feel how they appreciated it. I had never thought about working with firemen before.

INSIDE THE UNION SQUARE VIGIL
AN INTERVIEW WITH JORDAN SCHUSTER, THE 19 YEAR OLD COLLEGE KID WHO STARTED THE UNION SQUARE VIGIL, BY ACCIDENT.
William "Upski" Wimsatt

So what were you doing September 11?

I was sleeping and my roommate came into my room bawling in tears. Jordan, you have to get up. The World Trade Center has been attacked. I was still asleep. I'm a party promoter. I stay up late. It didn't even click in my head for a few minutes. But I have a really good friend who's an EMT and I knew she was gonna run down there and try to help. So I called her and she was like let's go.

We were walking downtown with a bunch of people who were trying to help and getting rejected. Everyone in the city was just walking around aimlessly. We were trying to figure out what to do.

I was writing my ideas down. I came up with an idea to do a mural like an AIDS quilt kind of thing. And I'm an event organizer, so I sent people on like six different errands. We went to Union Square and rolled out these two big pieces of butcher paper. People weren't congregating in Union Square yet or talking or anything. It was really strange. They were just walking around aimlessly.

So we put down the butcher paper and within 10 minutes, there were 50 people writing on it. Within an hour, there were 500. There'd be about 20 people writing at a time and other people were looking and they were crying and other people would come and say, "Do you need a hug?" And then someone would walk by and yell something like, "How can you people just sit there? We need to bomb some Arabs." And someone else would say, "That's not going to solve things." And it would start a political discussion. The papers were starting to fill up. I had my friends there I said we need four more rolls. It would take about an hour for each roll to get filled up. And the political discussions were popping up all over the place. And my friend James is a beautiful guy. He works in public housing and he would go in between the circles and create order, and institute a talking stick system, and then he'd delegate responsibility to people and then move on the next circle. And people got to know him, which was good because we would sometimes need to make announcements like "Here are ten organizations that need help right now," or "We need to pick up the trash." And then 16 women would offer to help.

All women?

For the most part! The men were helping with the arguing. Sometimes we saw people crossing over each others opinions. And we would say, "Hey, there's plenty of room. Be creative." Someone went around to all the messages that were like "We need revenge. Let's Go shoot em!" And they went to all the Ps and Ds and Os and drew flowers and butterflies and wrote "Let's use this emotion to grow something positive" or something along those lines. You could still read the message, but it was a creative response.

29

We started at about 3 pm on Tuesday. By the end of the day Tuesday, we had acquired about 20 volunteers and 35 sheets of butcher paper had been filled. There were people going around with markers saying, "Do you have anything you want to share?"

At 4 am the first night, there were about 50 people in the square. At 6am, people started coming. By 10 am there were 1000 people. By noon, there were 2000 people. Then we had at least 1000 people there all week. They wouldn't leave. We had close to 1000 people here at 3 am! Nobody had to go to work. People were saying thank you. I needed somewhere to go. I ran into like 30 friends I hadn't seen in forever. The vibe was so thick! You could butter your bread with the vibe that was there.

Yeah, I came on Thursday afternoon and it was so profound because I had been watching TV, and I was feeling horrible and sick. Watching TV, it seemed like the whole country wanted to nuke the Middle East.

You heard that 90% of the country was backing the President and literally no one from that other 10% was allowed to speak on TV. Congress had voted almost unanimously in favor of a blank check for war. So I come to Union Square, as close as you can get to Ground Zero. When I first got there and I saw people writing on the paper, after watching so much TV, I was almost dreading looking at what people were writing because I thought it was going to all be about bombing the Arabs, and it wasn't! I found it so heartening that almost all the messages were about peace. It was a miracle. It changed my whole feeling. I didn't feel sick anymore.

Union Square memorial
© Amy Woloszyn 2001

What was your experience with the media?

All the media came. ABC, CBS, NBC, Fox, the Warner Channel, New York One. But they all came with an agenda. They'd take shots of people crying and interview people saying, "We need to retaliate. We have all these weapons we're not even using. We need to blow some people up." The opinions being expressed were everything from peace and love to bloody revenge.

But predominantly, it was messages of peace, grief, and empathy. For every one pro-war and revenge sentiment, there were probably 15 pro-peace and understanding sentiments. Meanwhile, Friday night there were 10,000 people in Union Square holding a peace rally.

Unfortunately, that didn't get any coverage in the major media whatsoever. Well, NPR, PBS, and MTV did more balanced coverage, so did the BBC, but not the major networks.

I even asked them about it. On Saturday, CBS was there. I had started to notice that certain aspects of what was happening were not being covered and they were avoiding the predominant sentiment of the place which was peaceful, pro-humanity, pro-understanding sentiment. I'd say that for the last two weeks, at least 90% of the messages people have been expressing have been pro-peace, but the media was walking around looking for that other 10% that wanted vengeance. So I said to the CBS reporter: "I see you've been here for an hour and you haven't gone over and talked to those 200 people who've been singing 'Give Peace a Chance' since before you came. I'd say people were singing that song for a total of six hours. I don't see you interviewing these African drummers in the circle where I was just dancing for the last half hour with 150 other people where we just had Buddhist Monks performing love prayers. I notice you haven't taken pictures of that huge sign that says the quote from Gandhi." The reporter said something like: "We're not here to do that. That's not our agenda."

I stayed up in the park all night the first two nights. On the third day, it rained. We took all the papers and covered the stuff so it didn't get damaged. It was Biblical rain. I think it was symbolic for lots of people. A lot of the homeless people have African Djembes and Middle Eastern Tablas and started drumming under the subway covering. A lot of my friends and I danced in the rain.

We had the original conception, then it became its own thing. People were bringing their own paper, their own art projects, people were handing out free food, free water. By the sixth day, we weren't doing anything except handing out garbage bags and telling people to keep it clean. On Sunday, the city came and tried to take stuff away.

Trying to take away all the candles and flowers and signs and monuments???

Yeah, and everybody was protesting so they couldn't do it. It was four uniformed officers. So they came back at 6 am. They had to come back two mornings in a row. They put up these signs saying the stuff would be put in an archive. I would like to see that archive! I saw them putting it in the trash. People would come later that day and put down new candles and flowers and signs. This went on for a week and everyday, the Parks Department would clean it away.

But we saved the original 130 pieces of butcher paper. We're hoping to get them into a multi-media exhibit which travels to museums around the world. I spent maybe $200 on the whole thing. On paper and markers and food and duct tape.

31

NOT IN OUR SON'S NAME
Phyllis and Orlando Rodriguez

Our son Greg is among the many missing from the World Trade Center attack. Since we first heard the news, we have shared moments of grief, comfort, hope, despair, fond memories with his wife, the two families, our friends and neighbors, his loving colleagues at Cantor Fitzgerald / ESpeed, and all the grieving families that daily meet at the Pierre Hotel. We see our hurt and anger reflected among everybody we meet. We cannot pay attention to the daily flow of news about this disaster. But we read enough of the news to sense that our government is heading in the direction of violent revenge, with the prospect of sons, daughters, parents, friends in distant lands dying, suffering, and nursing further grievances against us. It is not the way to go. It will not avenge our son's death. Not in our son's name. Our son died a victim of an inhuman ideology. Our actions should not serve the same purpose. Let us grieve. Let us reflect and pray. Let us think about a rational response that brings real peace and justice to our world. But let us not as a nation add to the inhumanity of our times.

Ruben Shafer, Grandfather of Greg Rodriguez
© Margarita Garcia 2001

Copy of letter to White House:

Dear President Bush:
Our son is one of the victims of Tuesday's attack on the World Trade Center. We read about your response in the last few days and about the resolutions from both Houses, giving you undefined power to respond to the terror attacks. Your response to this attack does not make us feel better about our son's death. It makes us feel worse. It makes us feel that our government is using our son's memory as a justification to cause suffering for other sons and parents in other lands. It is not the first time that a person in your position has been given unlimited power and came to regret it. This is not the time for empty gestures to make us feel better. It is not the time to act like bullies. We urge you to think about how our government can develop peaceful, rational solutions to terrorism, solutions that do not sink us to the inhuman level of terrorists.

Sincerely,
Phyllis and Orlando Rodriguez

satellite photo of smoke rising from lower Manhattan
© Spaceimaging.com

33

"I know the towers are gone but like an amputee, I can't help but sense and feel and know that the ghost limbs of the twins are still there. But when I look up, as I did so often over the years to orient myself as to which way was south, I see that the twins are gone. It is a wound in the sky, and I feel it in my gut."

- Author unknown

SOME THAT MATTER

© Margarita Garcia 2001

"As a citizen, I have the right to represent a point of view. That's central to our democracy - the right to dissent, the right to provide a different point of view that's out in the open, in the full view of the American people."

- Rep Barbara Lee

```
From: Darryl Scipio
To: Jee Kim
Subject: RE: jeremy glick -FYI
```

```
jee,

this is a different jeremy glick. but our jeremy's
father was on the 64th floor of building 1 when the
first plane hit. he called his wife at 9:00 am to say
that a plane had hit, and we havent heard from him
since. jeremy's taking it kinda hard, so please keep him
in your prayers.
one.
```

I LOST MY BROTHER ON 9-11; DOES HE MATTER?

David Potorti, AlterNet
October 10, 2001

[Ed's note: On Tuesday, September 11, the writer lost his brother, James Potorti, at the World Trade Center. James worked on the 96th Floor of the first tower for a company called Marsh & McLennan.]

On October 8th, as most Americans rose concerned and curious about the military action taking place on the other side of the globe, NPR's Morning Edition host Bob Edwards asked Cokie Roberts to weigh in. "Leaders of Congress were quick to issue a statement in support of the military action in Afghanistan," he said. "Were there any dissenters?"

"None that matter," she replied.

It's a jaw-dropping statement when you think about it, one that says nothing and yet says everything.

But in a larger sense, of course, Roberts is right. In a media universe where you're as likely to find right-wing conservatives like Roberts on ABC, Fox, or NPR, the facts don't matter; only the framing. And in the hands of biased pundits posing as objective journalists, the framing is always going to be the same: pro-military, pro-government, and pro-war.

Still, Roberts may have done us a favor with her comment. Those three little words tell us worlds about the values informing the operation of US intelligence, the State Department, and the Pentagon. Understanding those words may bring us some much-needed clarity on US policies seemingly at odds with US values.

And let's not forget: it's a handy phrase you can use at home as well. Will network news divisions, owned by defense contractors, give us any useful insights into the workings of the US military? None that matter. Will you hear any coherent news reports from outside of a narrow, statist perspective? None that matter. And are there any mainstream media outlets willing to criticize US foreign policy? None that matter.

Thanks, Cokie. By telling us it doesn't matter, you've done more than express your biased political opinion. You've explained the arrogant, provincial, and value-free attitudes at work behind American foreign policy. And you've also given us valuable insight into the mindset of the terrorists behind the events of September 11.

Won't innocent American civilians die in the attacks? None that matter. Won't Islam be defamed in the eyes of other nations? None that matter. And, in the end, are the attacks likely to achieve much-needed changes in US foreign policy?

None that matter.

37

"We must not, out of anger and vengeance, indiscriminately retaliate in ways that bring on even more loss of innocent life."

- The National Council of Churches

A WIDOW'S PLEA FOR NON-VIOLENCE
Amber Amundson

My husband, Craig Scott Amundson of the US Army lost his life in the line of duty at the Pentagon on Sept. 11 as the world looked on in horror and disbelief. Losing my 28-year-old husband and father of our two young children is a terrible and painful experience. His death is also part of an immense national loss and I am comforted by knowing so many share my grief. But because I have lost Craig as part of this historic tragedy, my anguish is compounded exponentially by fear that his death will be used to justify new violence against other innocent victims.

I have heard angry rhetoric by some Americans, including many of our nation's leaders, who advise a heavy dose of revenge and punishment. To those leaders, I would like to make clear that my family and I take no comfort in your words of rage. If you choose to respond to this incomprehensible brutality by perpetuating violence against other innocent human beings, you may not do so in the name of justice for my husband. Your words and imminent acts of revenge only amplify our family's suffering, deny us the dignity of remembering our loved one in a way that would have made him proud, and mock his vision of America as a peacemaker in the world community.

Craig enlisted in the Army and was proud to serve his county. He was a patriotic American and a citizen of the world. Craig believed that by working from within the military system he could help to maintain the military focus on peacekeeping and strategic planning–to prevent violence and war. For the last two years Craig drove to his job at the Pentagon with a "visualize world peace" bumper sticker on his car. This was not empty rhetoric or contradictory to him, but part of his dream. He believed his role in the Army could further the cause of peace throughout the world. Craig would not have wanted a violent response to avenge his death. I ask our nation's leaders not to take the path that leads to more widespread hatreds–that make my husband's death just one more in an unending spiral of killing. I call on our national leaders to find the courage to respond to this incomprehensible tragedy by breaking the cycle of violence. I call on them to marshal this great nation's skills and resources to lead a worldwide dialogue on freedom from terror and hate.

"A lust for vengeance and violent retaliation is rising, fanned by a leader caught up in his own rhetoric of a holy war to purify the world of evil. Please consider: does the previous sentence describe bin Laden, or President Bush? If we pursue the path of large-scale violence, bin Laden's holy war and Bush's holy war will become two sides of the same war. "

- David R. Loy

CAN AMERICA HELP LEAD THE WORLD TO PEACE AND JUSTICE?
Greg Nees

Greg Nees wrote this letter to the president on September 13. As an afterthought he e-mailed it to friends and family who then forwarded it to their friends. Within a day it had traveled around the world and a suggestion was made to have it published in a major US newspaper. A campaign to make this possible began to organize itself among the readers of the letter.

While money and support came from more than 16 different countries, the strongest and most determined organizing force in this campaign was Yumi Kikuchi, a Japanese mother of four and environmental activist. Through her creative networking and untiring work, coupled with the enormous generosity of the Japanese people, it was possible to collect the $100,000 necessary for the ad within two weeks.

© Margarita Garcia 2001

The letter was published as a full page ad in the *New York Times* on October 9, the anniversary of John Lennon's birthday. Through the miracle of the human spirit and the wonders of the global internet, it was indeed possible to give peace a chance.

Dear Mr. President:

39

I am a former Marine Corps sergeant who served his country well and was honorably discharged in 1970. I have never written such a letter before and I hope that it will somehow reach you through the bureaucratic filters.

Like every other American, I was appalled by the death and destruction we witnessed September 11. We have suffered a horrible attack and far too many of us have suffered and died. Saddened and sickened by the carnage, I know you too are suffering with the victims and their families. I can feel your anger and frustration as well as your desire for active retaliation. I understand it well. It is a natural and justifiable reaction to such a heinous criminal act. And yet I would counsel you to proceed carefully. A mistake on our part could easily widen the spiral of violence.

Mr. President, you now have an historic opportunity to prove that the United States is more than just an economic and military power to be feared. You can show the world that the United States is also a civilized country that can be trusted to follow the law, guided by wisdom and compassion. I urge you to use all legal means at your disposal to determine who perpetrated this horrible crime and to bring them to trial before the appropriate court. Let them indeed find the justice the world awaits and needs.

"The US government and people should know that there is a vast difference between the poor and devastated people of Afghanistan and the terrorist Jehadi and Taliban criminals. While we once again announce our solidarity and deep sorrow with the people of the US, we also believe that attacking Afghanistan and killing its most ruined and destitute people will not in any way decrease the grief of the American people. We sincerely hope that the great American people could DIFFERENTIATE between the people of Afghanistan and a handful of fundamentalist terrorists. "

- Revolutionary Association of the Women of Afghanistan (RAWA)

But I beg you, let not one more innocent life-American, Israeli, Palestinian, Afghan or any other-be lost. Too often our weapons have taken the lives of innocents. The military euphemism is "collateral damage," but in reality it is manslaughter if not outright murder. What right can we claim that allows us to take more innocent lives? Is that not also a form of terrorism? Will we rise above the level of those who attacked us?

You have chosen to describe this as an act of evil. I fear using such language will only inflame the situation and incite a lynch mob mentality. What we need is compassion and cool reason to reach our true goals: peace, prosperity, and democracy for all peoples. Lead us, Mr. President, with dignity and wisdom. Show the world that you are a leader with the strength and courage to seek understanding and restorative justice, just as Nelson Mandela did in South Africa.

It is critical that we recognize not only the perpetrators willingness to use violence, but also the political and historical context in which this atrocity and their self-sacrifice has taken place.

As a former Marine, I know what it means to be willing to sacrifice one's life for a cause one truly believes in. Is it not possible that these people were simply horribly misguided, hate-filled and desperate, rather than cowardly or evil? If they see themselves as Davids fighting against a Goliath out to destroy their way of life, we certainly need not agree with them. But we must understand this point of view if we ever hope to achieve a lasting peace and avoid a world locked down and bereft of the rights and freedoms we cherish.

Months ago we saw unbearable images of a father and child helplessly pinned down in cross-fire. As a father yourself, can you imagine that parent's anguish as he felt the life ebb from his son? If we undertake military action which callously traps other families in cross-fire, anywhere in the world, we deaden what is most human within us.

This moment of deep crisis is also a moment of immense opportunity. I urge you to move our world away from violence and suffering and towards peace, freedom, and abundance for all. Bring the culpable to justice. But also let the voices of desperation be heard. Let us not repeat the mistake we did recently at the UN Conference on Racism in Durban, South Africa, but rather bring all voices to the table, even if they are screaming and telling the stories we do not want to hear.

We are truly a superpower, used to talking and expecting others to listen. Show the world that we are also strong enough to learn to listen. I pray that you will continue to resist the calls to rashly lash out in violence. May God give you the wisdom to find the opportunity that lies in this tragedy, for creating a lasting peace. I sincerely hope that future historians will look back at your actions and applaud the greatness of spirit and cool sense of reason that moved our world closer to justice and democracy for all.

41

Respectfully, Greg Nees
Former US Marine Sergeant

"Nations deny causality by ascribing blame to other terrorists, rogue nations, and so on. Singling out an enemy, we short-circuit the introspection necessary to see our own karmic responsibility for the terrible acts that have befallen us. Until we own causes we bear responsibility for, in this case in the Middle East, last week's violence will make no more sense than an earthquake or cyclone, except that in its human origin it turns us toward rage and revenge."

- The Buddhist Peace Fellowship

© Magarita Garcia, Burma, 1999

A LONE VOICE OF DISSENT
Davey D Talks to Rep. Barbara Lee
September 18, 2001

This interview with Rep. Barbara Lee was conducted by our friend Davey D,
editor of the excellent newsletter on Hip Hop and politics, FNV, at DaveyD.com.

*On Monday Sept 17th we had an opportunity to catch up with Congresswoman
Barbara Lee and talk to her about her decision to cast the only vote opposing
President Bush's War resolution. Not even her fellow colleagues from the
Congressional Black Caucus voted with her on this one. That includes such
notable people like Maxine Waters, Charles Rangel, Jesse Jackson Jr., Cynthia
McKinney to name a few. What is this all about? Is Congresswoman Lee out of
step with reality and the rest of the country? Or is she ahead of her time?*

DAVEY D: *They took this vote in Congress about what should be the response to
the tragedy this week... and elected to take military action. In a vote 420 to 1 you
were the lone dissenting voice that said no, we should not go to war.*

BARBARA LEE: First, our nation is in grieving, we're all mourning, we're angry;
there are a range of emotions taking place. Myself personally, I am also grieving
and I believe fully and firmly that the Congress of the United States is the only
legislative body that can say, "Let's pause for a moment...and let's look at
using some restraint before we rush to action." Because military action can
lead to an escalation and spiral out of control. So, why I voted no, was one, the
president already has the authority to execute a military action. He doesn't
need Congress - under the War Powers Act he has that authority. But Congress
is the people's house and is responsible for providing checks and balances,
and you cannot just allow the administration to run ahead with a strategy
without reporting back and without having some oversight. Now we must bring
the perpetrators to justice. International terrorism is upon us – this is a new
world and we cannot make any mistakes in dealing with it. We do not want to
see our reaction lead to another reaction which could allow this to spiral out of

control. So while we grieve and while we provide assistance – and I did vote to provide assistance for the families and communities that have been devastated and also providing funding for anti-terrorist activities for securing our own country – we've got to conduct a full investigation and be really deliberate about how we move forward militarily. We cannot make any mistake about this, this is an unconventional war and we have to fight it in an unconventional way.

DAVEY D: *We're talking about the nature of terrorism and whether it could be a tit-for-tat type of scenario if we go out and retaliate and hit the wrong targets or capture the wrong people, the next thing you know we could be involved in a situation where a can of worms has been opened that we just can't close it up.*

Selections from Hon Barbara Lee's statement in the House of Representatives Sept. 14, 2001.

Finally, we must be careful not to embark on an open-ended war with neither an exit strategy nor a focused target. We cannot repeat past mistakes.

In 1964, Congress gave President Lyndon Johnson the power to "take all necessary measures" to repel attacks and prevent further aggression. In so doing, this House abandoned its own constitutional responsibilities and launched our country into years of undeclared war in Vietnam.

At that time, Senator Wayne Morse, one of two lonely votes against the Tonkin Gulf Resolution, declared, "I believe that history will record that we have made a grave mistake in subverting and circumventing the Constitution of the United States...I believe that within the next century, future generations will look with dismay and great disappointment upon a Congress which is now about to make such a historic mistake." Senator Morse was correct, and I fear we make the same mistake today. And I fear the consequences.

43

BARBARA LEE: We don't know the real nature of terrorism in the true sense of the word. We have not invested in combating terrorism the way we should have, which involves many issues. It involves our foreign policy, it involves multinational cooperation, it involves diplomatic efforts. It involves pulling all of these very multifaceted areas together to come up with a real way to deal with terrorism. I don't believe we have faced the fact that terrorism is the new war that this country is going to have to fight. We're looking at putting up billions of dollars for national missile defense. Well, anti-ballistic missiles – that would not have saved the lives or prevented the horrible morning that we saw last Tuesday, it just wouldn't have done it. So, we're looking at putting military money into the wrong areas. We need to look at what this means in terms of securing our country, securing our world, and how to use our tax dollars toward that purpose. I am convinced that military action alone will not prevent further terrorist attacks.

Being patriotic at this moment in our history means participating in decisions about the future of our world. It means participating in decisions that will hopefully bring us to peace and ensure that these terrorists are brought to justice and that no man, woman, or child, ever gets killed in such brutal assaults ever again

CORNER TALK, SEPTEMBER
Danny Hoch

© Sophia Eminence 2001

1. hey yo son, i swear to god bee. i was standin outside mcdonalds kid, eatin a sausage and cheese mcmuffin, and i seen it happen son. at first i was like, what's that shadow? what's that shadow? then it was like boom, son. illuminati - nostradamus - dionne warwick type shit bee. you could still smell that shit in brooklyn son.

2. hey yo. bush was reading some dick and jane shit to some kids in florida, next thing you know, he told them kids - peace - got on his bulletproof plane and started makin zigzag type shit real quick. in his plane, talkin bout - they gonna kill me, they gonna kill me, go to nebraska, fuck it, go to alabama, go to china and shit. **running** yo. they had that cowboy crazy shook son.

3. my cousin was on the 90th floor and got out... word? My ex-girl was on the 61tst floor son. we aint heard from her still. that's the girl i was gonna marry yo. how was you gonna marry her but she's your ex? i know she's my ex, but still, we were gonna get married before, i'm saying. whatever bee, i just been blunted the whole week kid. i can't even think.

4. hey yo, i rented the siege last nite son. i swear to my mother george bush is

quoting bruce willis from the siege son. they had rounded up all the arabs and put em in some sprung shit, you know like internment camps in brooklyn, and i swear to my grandmother kid, bruce willis said, "make no mistake, we will hunt them down, we will find them, and we will wipe out evil in the world." rent that shit son! george bush said that shit 15 times this week. "make no mistake, we will do what bruce willis said in the siege.." he think he in a movie son! george bush think he fuckin bruce willis. he think colin powell is denzel washington. that shit is fucking crazy son.

"After seeing RAMBO last night, I know what to do the next time this happens."

- Ronald Reagan, as reported by *Daily Express*, July 2nd, 1985

5. hey yo- and people acting all scared. but not scared like you think though kid. i got a petition in my email. you know, one of those- stop bush from bombing the world type-emails. 60,000 people had signed that shit son by the time it got me. i was scrolling that shit down for like a hour and 20 minutes. but peep this - 40,000 people signed it "anonymous," that's how scared people are son. i don't know to be scared that they gonna setoff a bomb in my starbucks or that one of these flag-waving motherfuckers is gonna bomb ME for speakin my mind, you na mean? these flagheads is crazy son. i was talkin to this indian cat that just came here on vacation last week, he thought it was fuckin fouth of july kid. people actin all patriotic.

6. you wasnt patriotic when they was shootin amadou 41 times. or was you? you wasn't patriotic when they was shovin a broom handle in abner louima's ass, or when they was chokin anthony baez to death, or when they was shooting anthony rosario and anibal carrasquillo and frankie arzuaga in the **BACK**, on the **FLOOR**, or was you. why you lookin at me like that? something wrong? did i upset you? i didnt mean to **upset** you. you wasn't patriotic when bruce willis was stealing the fuckin election? or was you. tú sí tenías la bandera yanqui puesta mientras bombardeaban a vieques, es o no es? y ahora tú tá patriotico como carajo. you wasn't patriotic when we was bombing 200,000 iraquis, or when we were planting biological warfare in cuba, or when we were buying israel 7000 torture kits. or was you. or was you just... shook?

7. hey yo- but i aint scared yo, i aint scared. people on my block was **already** threatening to kill me man. cops too. my block **already** look like a plane hit it, word is bond son.

8. hey yo. but i dont understand kid, if there was 4 motherfuckers with box cutters on a plane, and I'M on the plane, they aint crashin **shit!** i'ma have to get cut or... somebody gonna have to get cut up. on some pizza shit. cause i aint goin out like that son. They say you cant bring knifes on planes now? i'ma bring a stick next time yo. somebody try to hijack the plane I'M on, they gonna catch multiple bumps kid. hardwood. you know that hardwood they make fancy chairs out of. i'ma go to macy's furniture department, or fuck it, i'ma go to huffman koos, and take a leg off of one of them expensive chairs, you know them overpriced shits they be sellin for like 6000 dollars, cause they had to go to brasil and kill the rainforest for that shit. i'ma break a leg off that one of them shits on the low, and fly anywhere. i'll fly to fuckin ohio or... oregon. and watch. let some motherfucker even say some shit to me son. cats is catchin **crazy** bumps kid. everybody in my aisle, i don't even care. like **WHAT**. but for real, i aint scared yo.

46

Anti-war, anti-racism rally, The Netherlands
© Michiel de Ruiter/www.wereldcrisis.nl, 2001

4. ricardo on the radio said in his accent thick as yuca, "i will

feel so much better when the first bombs drop over there. and my

friends feel the same way."

on my block, a woman was crying in a car parked and stranded in hurt.

i offered comfort, extended a hand she did not see before she said,

"we're gonna burn them so bad, i swear, so bad." my hand went to my

head and my head went to the numbers within it of the dead iraqi

children, the dead in nicaragua. the dead in rwanda who had to vie with fake sport wrestling for america's attention.

yet when people sent emails saying, this was bound to happen, lets

not forget US transgressions, for half a second i felt resentful.

hold up with that, cause i live here, these are my friends and fam,

and it could have been me in those buildings, and we're not bad

people, do not support america's bullying. can i just have a half

second to feel bad?

if i can find through this exhaust people who were left behind to

mourn and to resist mass murder, i might be alright.

thank you to the woman who saw me brinking my cool and blinking back

tears. she opened her arms before she asked "do you want a hug?" a

big white woman, and her embrace was the kind only people with the

warmth of flesh can offer. i wasn't about to say no to any comfort.

my brother's in the navy," i said. "and we're arabs". "wow, you

got double trouble." word.

- Suheir Hammad, "First Writing Since"

```
From: Jeremy Glick
To: Jee Kim
Subject: Re: good and bad


jee
thanks brother--you know i value all the support i've
gotten the most from my peeps--in music in
revolution...my dad is not making it, we don't have a
body yet and needless to say its been a nightmare. my
mom has been through hell and its not ending any time
soon. you guys have held me down and helped me when the
american media and patriotism has only made me sick and
convulse--to know that american imperialism is as we
speak pimping my father's death and others to
rationalize the impending slaughter adds a whole other
layer of disgust and dread to this very difficult
situation. the ONLY thing that has been keeping me up
and treading water for my mom is to know that folk like
you. i can not even begin to express how important that
has been for me. thanks jee for having my back. see
you soon kid.

jeremy
```

VIOLENT GANG COLORS
Statement from The Coup

Rapper and lyricist Boots Riley and DJ Pam the Funkstress, aka The Coup, would like to send their condolences to all who have been directly affected by the recent tragedy. Boots Riley offers this statement: "The similarity between the events of September 11, 2001 and the intended cover art for The Coup's new album, Party Music, is an unfortunate coincidence. The artwork was created in May of this year. The original intent of this artwork was to use the World Trade Center as a symbol of capitalism; the image was never meant to be taken literally, despite the uncanny similarity. All life is precious, and this tremendous tragedy is by no means taken lightly by The Coup. My condolences go out to the families and friends of the victims."

While the television media works the public into a venomous pro-war frenzy, however, it should be noted that a great number of similar atrocities have been committed by the US government and its corporate backers over the last few decades - many of which have caused a far greater loss of life than the recent bombings of New York and Washington DC.

With these terrible facts in mind, it is obvious that last week's events were symptomatic of a larger global backlash against US corporate imperialism. "The media would like to get angry at the faceless perpetrators of this crime and not the criminals with faces in the US government. We are encouraged to mourn the victims within our borders, and ignore the victims of US military actions in the rest of the world. What this fails to recognize is that the fear and sadness being felt now is the same fear and sadness that people in other countries have felt for years in their dealings with the US government... The Coup urges you to recognize all acts of terror and to realize that bombing Afghanistan or any other country will not address the root of this problem. It will simply cause the loss of more innocent lives. One last thing: The Coup does not support and has no respect for the American flag. It stands for oppression, exploitation, slavery, and murder. Which means if you're down with hip-hop, don't wave one. Hip-hop represents people fighting for freedom and justice. The American flag does not. No one will be admitted to a Coup show wearing red white and blue. They represent violent gang colors."

"That we demand quick and easy answers is indicative of our cultural attachment to instant gratification: got a headache, take an aspirin; overweight, get liposuction; upset about something, take Prozac. Don't think, don't analyze, just do it. It is Nike slogan as national mantra."

- Tim Wise

KEYNOTE SPEECH DELIVERED AT CAAAV'S 15TH ANNIVERSARY FUNDRAISER IN NEW YORK CITY

CAAAV organizes low-income Asian immigrant communities.
Angela Y. Davis
September 28, 2001

As the US flags wave against the backdrop of such evocative phrases as "we as a nation" and "we as Americans," (when what is really meant is "we as US citizens"), CAAAV compels us to respond in a way that moves beyond the easy and dangerous frame of US nationalism with its bellicose anthems and its hateful exclusion of those who are or appear to be non-citizens. This is a nationalism that requires leaders on which to displace the responsibility of national salvation.

So a major question for the people of this country — those who a few weeks ago were not so quick to accept George W. Bush as their leader (or New Yorkers not so quick to accept Guiliani as their leader) — is how to maintain a critical posture toward the current leadership. This requires us to maintain a critical historical memory. We have heard the media indicate many times that after September 11, things will never be the same. Yes, this is true — never again can we assume that the United States is invulnerable. But we cannot assume that everything has changed. The attack on the World Trade Center and on the Pentagon does not annul the history of US militarism. It does not cover up the fact that people of Japanese ancestry were held in internment camps during World War II. It does not diminish the meaning of war against Vietnam. And it should not camouflage the fact that the US significantly helped to create the conditions that led to the violence of Sept. 11. It should not blind us to the fact that — if Osama bin Laden is indeed the culprit and that if the Taliban is supporting him and his organization — that the US supported both bin Laden and the Taliban against

49

Man shouting, 'These colors don't run'
© Nick Cooper 2001

the former Soviet Union. It should not blind us to the fact that the US has refused to listen to the impassioned pleas of Afghan women who try to resist the patriarchal policies of the Taliban.

Why has George W. Bush suddenly emerged as a heroic figure, when not long ago, the results of the election were severely questioned all over the country and throughout the world? Thousands of innocent people were killed on Sept. 11 — and many of us have personal experience of this loss. Those of us who have no direct personal loss feel that we or our families and friends could have just as easily been among those who died. But this is a time to distinguish between the people of this country and the government and institutions that control the country. It is right to claim the innocence of those who died, but when we look at the governing institutions and leaders, we do not discover the same innocence.

The attack on Sept. 11 has been represented as an attack against global capitalism and the US flag as its symbol. But we must consider that many of those who died were already targets of the daily violence of global capitalism. This is not a time to wave the US flag, to claim the superiority of America and American citizens. This is not a time to claim the preeminence of Western Civilization as Italian Prime Minister Silvio Berlusconi did on Wednesday. In his words, according to the *New York Times*, "We should be confident of the superiority of our civilization, which consists of a value system that has given people widespread prosperity in those countries that embrace it and guarantees respect for human rights and religion." He went on to say that the West "is bound to occidentalize and conquer new people." Berlusconi also implicated the anti-globalization protesters in Genoa in a terrorist project linked to the violence of Sept. 11. What is important about Berlusconi's remarks is that he gave voice to the civilizational thinking that lurks about official discourse today. As the attack is described repeatedly as not just an attack against "America," but against "civilization," Bush makes reference to "smoking the terrorists out of holes" and "tracking them down in their caves."

This is why Dianne Feinstein feels justified in calling for a six-month moratorium on student visas. But let us not forget that that the so-called superiority of American freedom means oppression for people of the southern region and when convenient, it also excludes workers, citizens and non-citizens alike. The government is willing to bail out the airlines, but the airlines invoke their emergency clauses to avoid giving severance pay to laid off workers.

I want to suggest that we need to take our emotional responses seriously, that is we should understand them as emotional and not as the basis for foreign policy, not as the basis for new ways of thinking about entire populations, cultures and religions. Some of you may remember the initial responses to the bombing of the Oklahoma City Federal Building. In a recent interview in Z Magazine Noam Chomsky pointed out:

51

Into this neutral air

Where blind skyscrapers use

Their full height to proclaim

The strength of Collective Man,

Each language pours its vain

Competitive excuse:

But who can live for long

In an euphoric dream;

Out of the mirror they stare,

Imperialism's face

And the international wrong.

– W. H. Auden, "September 1, 1939"

"When a Federal Building was blown up in Oklahoma City, there were immediate cries to bomb the Middle East. These terminated when it was discovered that the perpetrator was from the US ultra-right militia movement. The reaction was not to destroy Montana and Idaho, where the movements are based, but to seek and capture the perpetrator, bring him to trial, and – crucially – explore the grievances that lie behind such crimes and to address the problems. Just about every crime – whether a robbery in the streets or colossal atrocities – has reasons, and commonly we find that some of them are serious and should be addressed. Matters are no different in this case — at least, for those who are concerned to reduce the threat of terrorist violence rather than to escalate it."

Although there have been many official pleas against racial profiling, there have also been innumerable attacks on people and institutions perceived to be associated with the individuals and organizations that may be responsible for the terrorist attacks in New York and Washington. Muslims, Arabs, South Asians have born the brunt of this racial profiling. Mosques have been attacked. South Asians have been murdered. People perceived to be of Middle Eastern descent have been removed from airplanes for no other reason than their physical appearance. This means that we will have to think more deeply about ways in which racism stimulates militarism and vice versa, how militarism promotes racism.

I must tell you that of the many thousands of candidates for whom I have ever voted in my life, there is one person who will always stand head and shoulders above all the rest. I voted for Barbara Lee to represent the congressional district in which I reside and I want to publicly congratulate her for having had the courage to stand up against militarism.

The use-of-force resolution passed 98-0 in the Senate and 420-1 in the House. Lee was the only person who voted against giving Bush a blank check for war. John Lewis said that "Several other members wanted to be there also but at the same time, like me, they didn't want to be seen as soft on terrorism."

Barbara Lee has reminded us that it is in precisely in times of crisis like this that we must hold on to our principles, that we should treasure our political memory. In this moment of intense communal mourning, we should be aware of the ease with which collective emotions can be politically manipulated toward ends that promote more violence and racism. Violence, as CAAAV points out, that will also be intensified by the INS — the federal agency that has more armed agents than any other, the FBI included. There are countless numbers of people of Middle Eastern descent who are currently being held by the INS, who have joined the thousands of others who languish in detention centers or jails and prisons. As the INS is a significant component of the prison industrial complex with evident links to the military industrial complex, it should be clearer than ever that prison activists need to join activists who work against racist immigration policy and practices.

In this context, I must mention the recent appointment of Tom Ridge to head the newly created "Office of Homeland Security." Imagine now that Condoleeza Rice and Tom Ridge and in charge of the security of the country. Ridge has signed more than 200 execution warrants since becoming governor of Pennsylvania in 1995, including two warrants for Mumia Abu-Jamal. The fascist resonances of this notion of "homeland security" should not be ignored, nor the fact that this is throwback to the internment camps for people of Japanese descent; and a throwback to the McCarthy era.

"Thousands of protesters 53 **peacefully flooded the streets of the nation's capital on Saturday to call for peace... Chanting 'War is not the answer,' an estimated 10,000 demonstrators assembled peacefully only blocks from the White House... Many of the protesters traveled from across the country to join the rally. James Creedon, a rescue worker in New York City, left the rubble of Ground Zero, where the World Trade Center once stood as a symbol of America's economic might, to join the medical teams at the protests."**

- Mark Wilkinson, *Reuters*

© Sophia Eminence 2001

The invocation of freedom as what the announced war against terrorism is designed to defend is the kind of ideology that has led historically to attacks on countless number of people — on their bodies and on their rights. When I hear the word "freedom" emanating from the mouth of Bush, from the mouths of Bushes, I ask — whose freedom and freedom toward what end? The market's freedom? Freedom to hire Filipina women at sub-minimum wage to provide domestic service for the affluent? Freedom to refuse to send a top-level delegation to the World Conference Against Racism? Freedom for the delegation to walk out of the conference and thus to refuse to help chart a global course to eradicate racism, including racism against Palestinians perpetrated by the Israeli government? Including reparations for the historical and current damage created by slavery? And by genocidal colonialist practices against indigenous peoples throughout the world.

This is not the kind of freedom most of us would want to support. If we wish today to look toward a world in which we can engage in the practice of freedom, the major question confronting us today is how to rebuild a strong anti-war movement with an equally strong anti-racist consciousness. In South Africa, at the World Conference Against Racism, many people learned that instead of looking toward the US government, they should look elsewhere in the US for leadership — to organizations like Third World Within, like the Women of Color Resource Center from the Bay Area (my own delegation) and, of course to CAAAV: Organizing Asian Immigrant Communities.

"Why of course the people don't want war. Why should some poor slob on a farm want to risk his life in a war when the best he can get out of it is to come back to his farm in one piece? Naturally the common people don't want war: neither in Russia, nor in England, nor for that matter in Germany. That is understood. But, after all, it is the leaders of the country who determine the policy and it is always a simple matter to drag the people along, whether it is a democracy, or a fascist dictatorship, or a parliament, or a communist dictatorship. Voice or no voice, the people can always be brought to the bidding of the leaders. That is easy. All you have to do is tell them they are being attacked, and denounce the peacemakers for lack of patriotism and exposing the country to danger. It works the same in any country. "

- Hermann Goering, Hitler's #2 Man

3

BLOWBACK

© Sebastião Salgado: Kabul, Afghanistan, 1996

"From the beginning, over the last 20 years, our entire Afghan policy has provided a reminder of the dangers of 'blowback,' a phrase used to describe the turning of the machinations of US intelligence agencies against our own nation."

- Robert Scheer, *Los Angeles Times*

"I think we can be reasonably confident that if the American population had the slightest idea of what is being done in their name, they would be utterly appalled."

- Noam Chomsky

INTERVIEW OF ZBIGNIEW BRZEZINSKI
Le Nouvel Observateur, Jan 15-21, 1998

Q: The former director of the CIA, Robert Gates, stated in his memoirs ("From the Shadows') that American intelligence services began to aid the Mujahadeen in Afghanistan 6 months before the Soviet intervention. In this period you were the national security adviser to President Carter. You therefore played a role in this affair. Is that correct?

Brzezinski: Yes. According to the official version of history, CIA aid to the Mujahadeen began during 1980, that is to say, after the Soviet army invaded Afghanistan, Dec 24, 1979. But the reality, secretly guarded until now, is completely otherwise: Indeed, it was July 3, 1979 that President Carter signed the first directive for secret aid to the opponents of the pro-Soviet regime in Kabul. And that very day, I wrote a note to the president in which I explained to him that in my opinion this aid was going to induce a Soviet military intervention.

Q: When the Soviets justified their intervention by asserting that they intended to fight against a secret involvement of the United States in Afghanistan, people didn't believe them. However, there was a basis of truth. You don't regret anything today?

B: Regret what? That secret operation was an excellent idea. It had the effect of drawing the Russians into the Afghan trap and you want me to regret it? The day that the Soviets officially crossed the border, I wrote to President Carter: We now have the opportunity of giving to the USSR its Vietnam war. Indeed, for almost 10 years, Moscow had to carry on a war unsupportable by the government, a conflict that brought about the demoralization and finally the breakup of the Soviet empire.

Q: And neither do you regret having supported the Islamic [intigrisme], having given arms and advice to future terrorists?

B: What is most important to the history of the world? The Taliban or the collapse of the Soviet empire? Some stirred-up Moslems or the liberation of Central Europe and the end of the cold war?

TEN THINGS TO KNOW ABOUT U.S. POLICY IN THE MIDDLE EAST

Stephen Zunes, AlterNet
September 26, 2001

1. THE UNITED STATES HAS PLAYED A MAJOR ROLE IN THE MILITARIZATION OF THE REGION.

The Middle East is the destination of the majority of American arms exports, creating enormous profits for weapons manufacturers and contributing greatly to the militarization of this already overly-militarized region. Despite promises of restraint, US arms transfers to the region have topped $60 billion since the Gulf War. Arms sales are an important component of building political alliances between the US and Middle Eastern countries, particularly with the military leadership of recipient countries. There is a strategic benefit for the US in having US-manufactured systems on the ground in the event of a direct US military intervention. Arms sales are also a means of supporting military industries faced with declining demand in Western countries.

To link arms transfers with a given country's human rights record would lead to the probable loss of tens of billions of dollars in annual sales for American weapons manufacturers, which are among the most powerful special interest groups in Washington. This may help explain why the United States has ignored the fact that UN Security Council resolution 687, which the US has cited as justification for its military responses to Iraq's possible rearmament, also calls for region-wide disarmament efforts, something the United States has rejected.

The US justifies the nearly $3 billion in annual military aid to Israel on the grounds of protecting that country from its Arab neighbors, even though the United States supplies 80 percent of the arms to these Arab states. The 1978 Camp David Accord between Israel and Egypt was in many ways more like a tripartite military pact than a peace agreement in that it has resulted in more than $5 billion is annual US arms transfers to those two countries. US weapons have been used repeatedly in attacks against civilians by Israel, Turkey and other countries. It is not surprising that terrorist movements have arisen in a region where so many states maintain their power influence through force of arms.

2. THE US MAINTAINS AN ONGOING MILITARY PRESENCE IN THE MIDDLE EAST.

The United States maintains an ongoing military presence in the Middle East, including longstanding military bases in Turkey, a strong naval presence in the eastern Mediterranean and Arabian Sea, as well as large numbers of troops on the Arabian Peninsula since the Gulf War. Most Persian Gulf Arabs and their leaders felt threatened after Iraq's seizure of Kuwait and were grateful for the strong US leadership in the 1991 war against Saddam Hussein's regime and for UN resolutions designed to curb Iraq's capability to produce weapons of mass destruction. At the same time, there is an enormous amount of cynicism regarding US motives in waging that war. Gulf Arabs, and even some of their rulers, cannot shake the sense that the war was not fought for international law, self-determination and human rights, as the senior Bush administration claimed, but rather to protect US access to oil and to enable the US to gain a strategic toehold in the region.

The ongoing US air strikes against Iraq have not garnered much support from the international community, including Iraq's neighbors, who would presumably be most threatened by an Iraqi capability of producing weapons of mass destruction. In light of Washington's tolerance – and even quiet support – of Iraq's powerful military machine in the 1980s, the United States' exaggerated claims of an imminent Iraqi military threat in 1998, after Iraq's military infrastructure was largely destroyed in the Gulf War, simply lack credibility. Nor have such recent air strikes eliminated or reduced the country's capability to produce weapons of mass destruction, particularly the most plausible threat of biological weapons.

Furthermore, only the United Nations Security Council has the prerogative to authorize military responses to violations of its resolutions; no single member state can do so unilaterally without explicit permission. Many Arabs object to the US policy of opposing efforts by Arabs states to produce weapons of mass destruction, while tolerating Israel's sizable nuclear arsenal and bringing US nuclear weapons into Middle Eastern waters as well as rejecting calls for the creation of a nuclear-free zone in the region.

In a part of the world which has been repeatedly conquered by outside powers of the centuries, this ongoing US military presence has created an increasing amount of resentment. Indeed, the stronger the US military role has become in the region in recent decades, the less safe US interests have become.

3. THERE HAS BEEN AN ENORMOUS HUMANITARIAN TOLL RESULTING FROM US POLICY TOWARD IRAQ.

Iraq still has not recovered from the 1991 war, during which it was on the receiving end of the heaviest bombing in world history, destroying much of the country's civilian infrastructure. The US has insisted on maintaining strict sanctions against Iraq to force compliance with international demands to dismantle any capability of producing weapons of mass destruction. In addition, the US hopes that such sanctions will lead to the downfall of Saddam Hussein's regime. However, Washington's policy of enforcing strict sanctions against Iraq appears to have had the ironic effect of strengthening Saddam's regime. With as many as 5,000 people, mostly children, dying from malnutrition and preventable diseases every month as a result of the sanctions, the humanitarian crisis has led to worldwide demands – even from some of Iraq's historic enemies – to relax the sanctions. Furthermore, as they are now more dependent than ever on the government for their survival, the Iraqi people are even less likely to risk open defiance.

"I think it's a time for questions. Why are people reaching the conclusions they're reaching in the Arab World? How are people in other countries seeing the lifestyles and the foreign policy of people in the US? Now it's not just critical for good politics. It's critical for survival."

- Drummond Pike, President, The Tides Foundation

Unlike the reaction to sanctions imposed prior to the war, Iraqi popular resentment over their suffering lays the blame squarely on the United States, not the totalitarian regime, whose ill-fated conquest of Kuwait led to the economic collapse of this once-prosperous country. In addition, Iraq's middle class, which would most likely have formed the political force capable of overthrowing Saddam's regime, has been reduced to penury. It is not surprising that most of Iraq's opposition movements oppose the US policy of ongoing punitive sanctions and air strikes.

In addition, US officials have stated that sanctions would remain even if Iraq complied with United Nations inspectors, giving the Iraqi regime virtually no incentive to comply. For sanctions to work, there needs to be a promise of relief to counterbalance the suffering; that is, a carrot as well as a stick. Indeed, it was the failure of both the United States and the United Nations to explicitly spell out what was needed in order for sanctions to be lifted that led to Iraq suspending its cooperation with UN weapons inspectors in December 1998.

4. THE UNITED STATES HAS NOT BEEN A FAIR MEDIATOR IN THE ISRAELI-PALESTINIAN CONFLICT.

For over two decades, the international consensus for peace in the Middle East has involved the withdrawal of Israeli forces to within internationally recognized boundaries in return for security guarantees from Israel's neighbors, the establishment of a Palestinian state in the West Bank and Gaza and some special status for a shared Jerusalem. Over the past 30 years, the Palestine Liberation Organization, under the leadership of Yasir Arafat, has evolved from frequent acts of terrorism and the open call for Israel's destruction to supporting the international consensus for a two-state solution. Most Arab states have made a similar evolution toward favoring just such a peace settlement.

© Julie Downey 2001

"Anti-Americanism in this context is not based on a hatred of modernity or technology-envy. It is based on a narrative of concrete interventions and specific depredations - the Iraqi people's suffering under US-imposed sanctions and US support for the 34-year-old Israeli occupation of Palestinian territories. Israel is now cynically exploiting the American catastrophe by intensifying its military occupation and oppression of the Palestinians."

- Edward Said

However, the US has traditionally rejected the international consensus and currently takes a position more closely resembling that of Israel's right-wing government: supporting a Jerusalem under largely Israeli sovereignty, encouraging only partial withdrawal from the occupied territories, allowing for the confiscation of Palestinian land and the construction of Jewish-only settlements and rejecting an independent state Palestine outside of Israeli strictures.

The interpretation of autonomy by Israel and the United States has thus far led to only limited Palestinian control of a bare one-fourth of the West Bank in a patchwork arrangement that more resembles American Indian reservations or the infamous Bantustans of apartheid-era South Africa than anything like statehood. The US has repeatedly blamed the Palestinians for the violence of the past year, even though Amnesty International, Human Rights Watch and other reputable human rights group have noted that the bulk of the violence has come from Israeli occupation forces and settlers.

Throughout the Israeli-Palestinian peace process, the US has insisted on the two parties working out a peace agreement among themselves, even though there has always been a gross asymmetry in power between the Palestinians and their Israeli occupiers. The US has blamed the Palestinians for not compromising further, even though they already ceded 78 percent of historic Palestine to the Israelis in the Oslo Accords; the Palestinians now simply demand that the Israelis withdraw their troops and colonists only from lands seized in the 1967, which Israel is required to do under international law.

The US-backed peace proposal by former Israeli prime minister Ehud Barak at the 2000 talks at Camp David would have allowed Israel to annex large swaths of land in the West Bank, control of most of Arab East Jerusalem and its environs, maintain most of the illegal settlements in a pattern that would have divided the West Bank into non-contiguous cantons, and deny Palestinian refugees the right of return. With the US playing the dual role of the chief mediator of the conflict as well as the chief diplomatic, financial and military backer of Israeli occupation forces, the US goal seems to be more that of Pax Americana than that of a true peace.

5. US SUPPORT FOR ISRAEL OCCUPATION FORCES HAS CREATED ENORMOUS RESENTMENT THROUGHOUT THE MIDDLE EAST.

The vast majority of Middle Eastern states and their people have belatedly acknowledged that Israel will continue to exist as part of the region as an independent Jewish state. However, there is enormous resentment at ongoing

US diplomatic, financial and military support for Israeli occupation forces and their policies.

The US relationship with Israel is singular. Israel represents only one one-thousandth of the world's population and has the 16th highest per capita income in the world, yet it receives nearly 40 percent of all US foreign aid. Direct aid to Israel in recent years has exceeded $3.5 billion annually, with an additional $1 billion through other sources, and has been supported almost unanimously in Congress, even by liberal Democrats who normally insist on linking aid to human rights and international law. Although the American public appears to strongly support Israel's right to exist and wants the US to be a guarantor of that right, there is growing skepticism regarding the excessive level and unconditional nature of US aid to Israel. Among elected officials, however, there are virtually no calls for a reduction of current aid levels in the foreseeable future, particularly as nearly all US aid to Israel returns to the United States either via purchases of American armaments or as interest payments to US banks for previous loans.

Despite closer American strategic cooperation with the Persian Gulf monarchies since the Gulf War, these governments clearly lack Israel's advantages in terms of political stability, a well-trained military, technological sophistication and the ability to quickly mobilize human and material resources.

Despite serious reservations about Israel's treatment of the Palestinians, most individual Americans have a longstanding moral commitment to Israel's survival.

```
To: Jeremy Glick
From: Jee Kim
Subject: stay up

Glad to hear you're maintaining through all this. I know
all this talk of war isn't helping.
```

```
To: Jee Kim
From: Jeremy Glick
Subject: Re: stay up

To say the least.

I'm at home with my family in a premature, "House of
Mourning" listening to the pundits on the TV talk about
further enabling the CIA when they were the
motherfuckers who got us into this mess w/ bin Laden.
That republican sector of the ruling class, with Bush
Sr. as director of the CIA, provided the momentum,
military training, and economic backing of the network
that allegedly killed my father. Now they want to sit
back and claim righteous indignation while they lock up
all my friends for bullshit nickel bag of smoke charges
```

Official US government policy supporting successive Israeli governments in recent years, however, appears to be crafted more from a recognition of how Israel supports American strategic interests in the Middle East and beyond. Indeed, 99 percent of all US aid to Israel has been granted since the 1967 war, when Israel proved itself more powerful than any combination of its neighbors and occupied the territories of hundreds of thousands of Palestinians and other Arabs. Many Israelis supportive of that country's peace movement believe the United States has repeatedly undermined their efforts to moderate their government's policies, arguing that Israeli security and Palestinian rights are not mutually-exclusive, as the US seems to believe, but mutually dependent on the other.

© Julie Downey 2001

As long as US military, diplomatic and economic support of the Israeli government remains unconditional despite Israel's ongoing violation of human rights, international law and previous agreements with the Palestinians, there is no incentive for the Israeli government to change its policies. The growing Arab resentment that results can only threaten the long-term security interests of both Israel and the United States.

63

6. THE UNITED STATES HAS BEEN INCONSISTENT IN ITS ENFORCEMENT OF INTERNATIONAL LAW AND UN SECURITY COUNCIL RESOLUTIONS.

The US has justified its strict sanctions and ongoing air strikes against Iraq on the grounds of enforcing United Nations Security Council resolutions. In addition, in recent years the United States has successfully pushed the UN Security Council to impose economic sanctions against Libya, Afghanistan and Sudan over extradition disputes, an unprecedented use of the UN's authority. However, the US has blocked sanctions against such Middle East allies as Turkey, Israel and Morocco for their ongoing occupation of neighboring countries, far more egregious violations of international law that directly counter the UN Charter. In recent years, for example, the US has helped block the Security Council from moving forward with a UN-sponsored resolution on the fate of the Moroccan-occupied country of Western Sahara because of the likelihood that the people would vote for independence from Morocco, which invaded the former Spanish colony with US backing in 1975.

Over the past 30 years, the US has used its veto power to protect its ally Israel from censure more than all other members of the Security Council have used their veto power on all other issues combined. This past spring, for example, the US vetoed an otherwise-unanimous resolution which would have dispatched unarmed human rights monitors to the Israeli-occupied West Bank and Gaza Strip. In addition, the US has launched a vigorous campaign to rescind all previous UN resolutions critical of Israel. Washington has labeled them "anachronistic," even though many of the issues addressed in these resolutions – human rights violations, illegal settlements, expulsion of dissidents, development of nuclear weapons, the status of Jerusalem, and ongoing military occupation – are still germane. The White House contends that the 1993 Oslo Accords render these earlier UN resolutions obsolete. However, such resolutions cannot be reversed without the approval of the UN body in question; the US cannot unilaterally discount their relevance. Furthermore, no bilateral agreement (like Oslo) can supersede the authority of the UN Security Council, particularly if one of the two parties (the Palestinians) believe that these resolutions are still binding.

"The important thing to remember is that when it happens to others it's collateral damage, when they do it to us it's terrorism."

-Manas Chakravarty

Most observers recognize that one of the major obstacles to Israeli-Palestinian peace is the expansion of Israeli settlements in the occupied territories. However, the US has blocked enforcement of UN Security Council resolutions calling for Israel to withdraw its settlements from Palestinian land. These settlements were established in violation of international law, which forbids the colonization of territories seized by military force. In addition, the US has not opposed the expansion of existing settlements and has shown ambivalence regarding the large-scale construction of exclusively Jewish housing developments in Israeli-occupied East Jerusalem. Furthermore, the US has secured additional aid for Israel to construct highways connecting these settlements and to provide additional security, thereby reinforcing their permanence. This places the United States in direct violation of UN Security Council resolution 465, which "calls upon all states not to provide Israel with any assistance to be used specifically in connection with settlements in the occupied territories."

7. THE UNITED STATES HAS SUPPORTED AUTOCRATIC REGIMES IN THE
MIDDLE EAST.

The growing movement favoring democracy and human rights in the Middle East
has not shared the remarkable successes of its counterparts in Eastern
Europe, Latin America, Africa and parts of Asia. Most Middle Eastern
governments remain autocratic. Despite occasional rhetorical support for
greater individual freedoms, the United States has generally not supported
tentative Middle Eastern steps toward democratization. Indeed, the United
States has reduced – or maintained at low levels – its economic, military and
diplomatic support to Arab countries that have experienced substantial political
liberalization in recent years while increasing support for autocratic regimes
such as Saudi Arabia, Kuwait, Egypt and Morocco. Jordan, for example, received
large-scale US support in the 1970s and 1980s despite widespread repression
and authoritarian rule; when it opened up its political system in the early
1990s, the US substantially reduced – and, for a time, suspended – foreign aid.
Aid to Yemen was cut off within months of the newly unified country's first
democratic election in 1990.

65

"Let's expose to public scrutiny, which Presidents of the US, Secretaries of Defense, and CIA officers decided to train and support bin Laden. I want to hear former and current US officials publicly apologize."

- Steven Feuerstein, Not In My Name (Chicago)

Despite its laudable rhetoric, Washington's real policy regarding human rights in
the Middle East is not difficult to infer. It is undeniable that democracy and
universally recognized human rights have never been common in the Arab-
Islamic world. Yet the tendency in the US to emphasize cultural or religious
explanations for this fact serves to minimize other factors that are arguably
more salient – including the legacy of colonialism, high levels of militarization
and uneven economic development – most of which can be linked in part to the
policies of Western governments, including the United States. There is a
circuitous irony in a US policy that sells arms, and often sends direct military
aid, to repressive Middle Eastern regimes that suppress their own people and
crush incipient human rights movements, only to then claim that the resulting
lack of democracy and human rights is evidence that the people do not want
such rights. In reality, these arms transfers and diplomatic and economic
support systems play an important role in keeping autocratic Arab regimes in

power by strengthening the hand of the state and supporting internal repression. The US then justifies its large-scale military aid to Israel on the grounds that it is "the sole democracy in the Middle East," even though these weapons are used less to defend Israeli democracy than to suppress the Palestinians' struggle for self-determination.

8. US POLICY HAS CONTRIBUTED TO THE RISE OF RADICAL ISLAMIC GOVERNMENTS AND MOVEMENTS.

The United States has been greatly concerned in recent years over the rise of radical Islamic movements in the Middle East. Islam, like other religions, can be quite diverse regarding its interpretation of the faith's teachings as they apply to contemporary political issues. There are a number of Islamic-identified parties and movements that seek peaceful coexistence and cooperation with the West and are moderate on economic and social policy. Many Islamist movements and parties have come to represent mainstream pro-democracy and pro-economic justice currents, replacing the discredited Arab socialism and Arab nationalist movements.

There are also some Islamic movements in the Middle East today that are indeed reactionary, violent, misogynist and include a virulently anti-American perspective that is antithetical to perceived American interests. Still others may be more amenable to traditional US interests but reactionary in their approach to social and economic policies, or vice versa.

Such movements have risen to the forefront primarily in countries where there has been a dramatic physical dislocation of the population as a result of war or uneven economic development. Ironically, the United States has often supported policies that have helped spawn such movements, including giving military, diplomatic and economic aid to augment decades of Israeli attacks and occupation policies, which have torn apart Palestinian and Lebanese society, and provoked extremist movements that were unheard of as recently as 20 years ago. The US-led overthrow of the constitutional government in Iran in 1953 and subsequent support for the Shah's brutal dictatorship succeeded in crushing that country's democratic opposition, resulting in a 1979 revolution led by hard-line Islamic clerics. The United States actually backed extremist Islamic groups in Afghanistan when they were challenging the Soviet Union in the 1980s, including Osama bin Laden and many of his followers. To this day, the United States maintains very close ties with Saudi Arabia, which despite being labeled a "moderate" Arab regime, adheres to an extremely rigid interpretation of Islam and is among the most repressive regimes in the world.

9. THE US PROMOTION OF A NEO-LIBERAL ECONOMIC MODEL IN THE MIDDLE EAST HAS NOT BENEFITED MOST PEOPLE OF THE REGION.

Like much of the Third World, the United States has been pushing a neo-liberal economic model of development in the Middle East through such international financial institutions as the International Monetary Fund, the World Bank and the World Trade Organization. These have included cutbacks in social services, encouragement of foreign investment, lower tariffs, reduced taxes, the elimination of subsidies for farmers and basic foodstuffs as well as ending protection for domestic industry.

While in many cases, this has led to an increase in the overall Gross National Product, it has dramatically increased inequality, with only a minority of the population benefiting. Given the strong social justice ethic in Islam, this growing disparity between the rich and the poor has been particularly offensive to Muslims, whose exposure to Western economic influence has been primarily through witnessing some of the crassest materialism and consumerism from US imports enjoyed by the local elites.

67

Widow
© Sebastião Salgado, Beharke, Iraqi Kurdistan, 1997

The failure of state-centric socialist experiments in the Arab world have left an ideological vacuum among the poor seeking economic justice which has been filled by certain radical Islamic movements. Neo-liberal economic policies have destroyed traditional economies and turned millions of rural peasants into a new urban underclass populating the teeming slums of such cities as Cairo, Tunis, Casablanca and Teheran. Though policies of free trade and privatization have resulted in increased prosperity for some, far more people have been left behind, providing easy recruits for Islamic activists rallying against corruption, materialism and economic injustice.

10. THE US RESPONSE TO MIDDLE EASTERN TERRORISM HAS THUS FAR BEEN COUNTER-PRODUCTIVE.

The September 11 terrorist attacks on the United States has highlighted the threat of terrorism from the Middle East, which has become the country's major national security concern in the post-cold war world. In addition to Osama bin Laden's underground Al-Qaeda movement, which receives virtually no direct support from any government, Washington considers Iran, Iraq, Sudan and Libya to be the primary sources of state-sponsored terrorism and has embarked on an ambitious policy to isolate these regimes in the international community. Syria's status as a supporter of terrorism has ebbed and flowed not so much from an objective measure of its links to terrorist groups as from an assessment of their willingness to cooperate with US policy interests, indicating just how politicized "terrorist" designations can be.

Responding to terrorist threats through large-scale military action has been counter-productive. In 1998, the US bombed a civilian pharmaceutical plant in Sudan under the apparently mistaken belief that it was developing chemical weapons that could be used by these terrorist networks, which led to a wave of anti-Americanism and strengthened that country's fundamentalist dictatorship. The 1986 bombing of two Libyan cities in response to Libyan support for terrorist attacks against US interests in Europe not only killed scores of civilians, but – rather than curb Libyan-backed terrorism – resulted in Libyan agents blowing up a Pan Am airliner over Scotland in retaliation. Military responses generally perpetuate a cycle of violence and revenge. Furthermore, failure to recognize the underlying grievances against US Middle East policy will make it difficult to stop terrorism. While very few Muslims support terrorism – recognizing it as contrary to the values of Islam – the concerns articulated by bin Laden and others about the US role in the region have widespread resonance and will likely result in new recruits for terrorist networks unless and until the US changes its policies.

Over the past two decades, the US has bombed Lebanon, Iran, Sudan, and Afghanistan in an effort to challenge Islamic movements and governments viewed as antithetical to US interests. Such air strikes have not only been contrary to international law but have also resulted in fueling anti-American hatred, particularly when they have caused civilian casualties.

Trying to impose military solutions to what are essentially political, economic, and social problems is doomed to fail.

```
To: Jeremy Glick
From: Jee Kim
Subject: cruelty

Does it surprise you? I mean, looking at history, how
does the blood on ban Laden's hands (if he is
responsible for the Sept 11 attacks) compare to that on
say, Kissinger's?

Btw, look at this great quote I found:
"I believe that if we had and would keep our dirty,
bloody, dollar soaked fingers out of the business of
these (Third World) nations, so full of depressed,
exploited people, they will arrive at a solution of
their own. And if unfortunately their revolution must be
of the violent type because the "haves" refuse to share
with the "have-nots" by any peaceful method, at least
what they get will be their own, and not the American
style, which they don't want and above all don't want
crammed down their throats by Americans." -General David
Sharp (Former United States Marine Commandant 1966)
```

69

TOWARD A NEW FOREIGN POLICY

The US must shift from supporting repressive governments to encouraging greater democracy and pluralism in the Islamic world. The US must demand an end to Israel's illegal occupation of Arab East Jerusalem and other Palestinian territories and promote a peace agreement that recognizes the city's importance to all three monotheistic faiths. The US should support sustainable economic development in the Islamic world, so that the benefits of foreign investment and globalization can be more fairly distributed with minimal social disruption.

To effectively challenge the threat from radical Islamic movements, the US must shift its focus from trying to crush such movements to pursuing policies that discourage their emergence. Similarly, the US must recognize that not all Islamic movements are contrary to the development of political pluralism or good relations with the United States.

From Afghanistan to Algeria and beyond, radical Islamic movements have grown to prominence where there has been great social dislocation in the population, whether it be from war or misguided economic policies. Policies designed to minimize such traumatic events will be far more successful than military threats in encouraging moderation in Islamic countries.

The US must cease its support for autocratic regimes and encourage greater political pluralism. In countries like Jordan, Turkey, and Yemen, where Islamic parties have been allowed to compete in a relatively open political process, they have generally played a responsible – if somewhat conservative – role in the political system. The more radical elements observable in many Islamic movements are usually a reflection of the denial of their right to participate in political discourse. Many radical Islamic movements, such as those in Egypt, Palestine, and Algeria, include diverse elements. Were they no longer under siege and instead allowed to function in an open democratic system they would likely divide into competing political parties ranging across the ideological spectrum...

Indeed, no extremist Islamic movements have ever evolved in democratic societies. Supporting democracy would therefore be a major step in the direction of moderating political Islam. The US must stop considering Islam to be the enemy and instead encourage Islamic movements by working for justice and economic equality.

Washington must support the Palestinians' right to statehood in the West Bank and Gaza, including a shared Jerusalem that would serve as the capital of both Israel and Palestine. Both Congress and the executive branch should rescind resolutions and past statements that imply support for Israel's unilateral annexation of Arab East Jerusalem and surrounding Palestinian lands. Washington must instead recognize the city's importance to all three monotheistic faiths. Not only would such a policy shift bring the US in line with international law, UN Security Council resolutions, and virtually the entire international community, but it would also remove a highly emotional and volatile issue from the arsenal of Islamic extremists, who exploit the widespread anger about US support for the illegal Israeli occupation of a city that Muslims also see as holy.

The US should stop pushing for radical economic liberalization in Islamic countries, since such policies increase inequality and result in rising materialism and conspicuous consumption for elites at the expense of basic needs of the poor majority. Instead, the US must support sustainable economic development, so that the benefits of foreign investment and globalization can be more fairly distributed with minimal social disruption. Although some Islamic traditions have proven to be relatively tolerant of autocratic governance, the presence of corruption and a lack of concern about social injustice by a country's leadership are generally seen by Muslims as a violation of a social contract and must be resisted.

In many respects, political Islam has filled a vacuum that resulted from the failure of Arab nationalism, Marxism, and other ideologies to free Islamic countries both from unjust political, social, and economic systems and from Western imperialism. Just because radical Islamic movements have embraced tactics and ideologies reprehensible to most Westerners does not mean that the concerns giving rise to such movements are without merit.

Only by addressing the legitimate grievances of these movements will there be any hope of stopping their often illegitimate methods and questionable ideologies. Otherwise, the US may find itself dealing with a series of conflicts that could eclipse the bloody surrogate cold war battles that ravaged the third world in previous decades.

"There's something absurd in the sentiment of congressional leaders, who the *New York Times* reported Sunday ' have concluded that American spy agencies should be allowed to combat terrorism with more aggressive tactics, including the hiring of unsavory foreign agents.' When did the CIA stop hiring 'unsavory' agents?"

71

- Robert Scheer, *Los Angeles Times*

SHOCKED AND HORRIFIED
Larry Mosqueda, Ph.D.

Like all Americans, on Tuesday, 9-11, I was shocked and horrified to watch the WTC Twin Towers attacked by hijacked planes and collapse, resulting in the deaths of perhaps up to 10,000 innocent people.

I had not been that shocked and horrified since January 16, 1991, when then President Bush attacked Baghdad, and the rest of **Iraq** and began killing **200,000** people during that "war" (slaughter). This includes the infamous "highway of death" in the last days of the slaughter when US pilots literally shot in the back retreating Iraqi civilians and soldiers. I continue to be horrified by the sanctions on Iraq, which have resulted in the death of over **1,000,000 Iraqis**, including over 500,000 children, about whom former Secretary of State Madeleine Albright has stated, their deaths "are worth the cost."

Over the course of my life I have been shocked and horrified by a variety of US governmental actions, such as the US sponsored coup against democracy in

Guatemala in 1954 which resulted in the deaths of over **120,000 Guatemalan** peasants by US installed dictatorships over the course of four decades. Last Tuesday's events reminded me of the horror I felt when the US overthrew the government of the **Dominican Republic** in 1965 and helped to murder **3,000** people. And it reminded me of the shock I felt in 1973, when the US sponsored a coup in **Chile** against the democratic government of Salvador Allende and helped to murder another **30,000** people, including US citizens.

Last Tuesday's events reminded me of the shock and horror I felt in 1965 when the US sponsored a coup in **Indonesia** that resulted in the murder of over **800,000** people, and the subsequent slaughter in 1975 of over **250,000** innocent people in **East Timor** by the Indonesian regime, with the direct complicity of President Ford and Secretary of State Henry Kissinger.

I was reminded of the shock and horror I felt during the US sponsored terrorist contra war (the World Court declared the US government a war criminal in 1984 for the mining of the harbors) against **Nicaragua** in the 1980s which resulted in the deaths of over **30,000** innocent people (or as the US government used to call them before the term "collateral damage" was invented–"soft targets").

"In 1996, Madeleine Albright, then the US secretary of state, was asked on national television what she felt about the fact that 500,000 Iraqi children had died as a result of US economic sanctions. She replied that it was 'a very hard choice,' but that, all things considered, 'we think the price is worth it.' "

- Arundhati Roy

I was reminded of being horrified by the U. S. war against the people of **El Salvador** in the 1980s, which resulted in the brutal deaths of over **80,000** people, or "soft targets."

I was reminded of the shock and horror I felt during the US sponsored terror war against the peoples of southern Africa (especially **Angola**) that began in the 1970s and continues to this day, and has resulted in the deaths and mutilations of over **1,000,000**. I was reminded of the shock and horror I felt as the US invaded Panama over the Christmas season of 1989 and killed over **8,000** in an attempt to capture George H. Bush's CIA partner, now turned enemy, Manuel Noriega.

I was reminded of the horror I felt when I learned about how the Shah of Iran was installed in a US sponsored brutal coup that resulted in the deaths of over **70,000 Iranians** from 1952-1979. And the continuing shock as I learned that the Ayatollah Khomani, who overthrew the Shah in 1979, and who was the US public enemy for the decade of the 1980s, was also on the CIA payroll while he was in exile in Paris in the 1970s.

I was reminded of the shock and horror that I felt as I learned about the how the US has "manufactured consent" since 1948 for its support of Israel, to the exclusion of virtually any rights for the Palestinians in their native lands resulting in ever worsening day-to-day conditions for the people of **Palestine**. I was shocked as I learned about the hundreds of towns and villages that were literally wiped off the face of the earth in the early days of Israeli colonization. I was horrified in 1982 as the villagers of Sabra and Shatila were massacred by Israeli allies with direct Israeli complicity and direction. The **untold thousands** who died on that day match the scene of horror that we saw last Tuesday. But those scenes were not repeated over and over again on the national media to inflame the American public.

73

The events and images of last Tuesday have been appropriately compared to the horrific events and images of Lebanon in the 1980s with resulted in the deaths of tens of thousand of people, with no reference to the fact that the country that inflicted the terror on Lebanon was Israel, with US backing. I still continue to be shocked at how mainstream commentators refer to "Israeli settlers" in the "occupied territories" with no sense of irony as they report on who are the aggressors in the region.

Of course, the largest and most shocking war crime of the second half of the 20th century was the US assault on Indochina from 1954-1975, especially **Vietnam**, where over **4,000,000** people were bombed, napalmed, crushed, shot and individually "hands on" murdered in the "Phoenix Program" (this is where Oliver North got his start). Many US Vietnam veterans were also victimized by this war and had the best of intentions, but the policy makers themselves knew the criminality of their actions and policies as revealed in their own words in "The Pentagon Papers," released by Daniel Ellsberg of the RAND Corporation. In 1974 Ellsberg noted that our Presidents from Truman to Nixon continually lied to the US public about the purpose and conduct of the war. He has stated that, "It is a tribute to the American people that our leaders perceived that they had to lie to us, it is not a tribute to us that we were so easily misled." I was continually shocked and horrified as the US attacked and bombed with impunity the nation of Libya in the 1980s, including killing the infant daughter of Khadafi. I was shocked as the US bombed and invaded **Grenada** in 1983. I was horrified by US military and CIA actions in **Somalia, Haiti, Afghanistan,**

Sudan, Brazil, Argentina, and Yugoslavia. The deaths in these actions ran into the hundreds of thousands.

The above list is by no means complete or comprehensive. It is merely a list that is easily accessible and not unknown, especially to the economic and intellectual elites. It has just been conveniently eliminated from the public discourse and public consciousness. And for the most part, the analysis that the US actions have resulted in the deaths of primarily civilians (over 90%) is not unknown to these elites and policy makers. **A conservative number for those who have been killed by US terror and military action since World War II is 8,000,000 people. Repeat–8,000,000 people.** This does not include the wounded, the imprisoned, the displaced, the refugees, etc. Martin Luther King, Jr. stated in 1967, during the Vietnam War, "My government is the world's leading purveyor of violence." Shocking and horrifying.

Nothing that I have written is meant to disparage or disrespect those who were victims and those who suffered death or the loss of a loved one during this week's events. It is not meant to "justify" any action by those who bombed the Twin Towers or the Pentagon. It is meant to put it in a context.

Ed Herman in his book *The Real Terror Network: Terrorism in Fact and Propaganda* does not justify any terrorism but points out that states often engage in "wholesale" terror, while those whom governments define as "terrorist" engage in "retail" terrorism. While qualitatively the results are the same for the individual victims of terrorism, there is a clear quantitative difference. And as Herman and others point out, the seeds, the roots, of much of the "retail" terror are in fact found in the "wholesale" terror of states. Again this is not to justify, in any way, the actions of last Tuesday, but to put them in a context and suggest an explanation...

The retail terror is that of desperate and sometimes fanatical small groups and individuals who often have legitimate grievances, but engage in individual criminal and illegitimate activities; the wholesale terror is that of "rational" educated men where the pain, suffering, and deaths of millions of people are contemplated, planned, and too often, executed, for the purpose of furthering a nebulous concept called the "national interest." Space does not allow a full explanation of the elites' Orwellian concept of the "national interest," but it can be summarized as the protection and expansion of hegemony and an imperial empire.

The American public is being prepared for war while being fed a continuous stream of shocking and horrific repeated images of Tuesday's events, and heartfelt stories from the survivors and the loved ones of those who lost family members. These stories are real and should not be diminished. In fact, those who lost family members can be considered a representative sample of humanity of the 8,000,000 who have been lost previously. If we multiply by 800-1000 times the amount of pain, angst, and anger being currently felt by the American public, we might begin to understand how much of the rest of the world feels as they are continually victimized.

Some particularly poignant images are the heart wrenching public stories that we are seeing and hearing of family members with pictures and flyers searching for their loved ones. These images are virtually the same as those of the "Mothers of the Disappeared" who searched for their (primarily) adult children in places such as **Argentina**, where over **11,000** were "disappeared" in 1976-1982, again with US approval. Just as the mothers of Argentina deserved our respect and compassion, so do the relatives of those who are searching for their relatives now. However we should not allow ourselves to be manipulated by the media and US government into turning real grief and anger into a national policy of wholesale terror and genocide against innocent civilians in Asia and Africa. What we are seeing in military terms is called "softening the target." The target here is the American public and we are being ideologically and emotionally prepared for the slaughter that may commence soon...

75

Those affected, all of us, must do everything in our power to prevent a wider war and even greater atrocity, do everything possible to stop the genocide if it starts, and hold those responsible for their potential war crimes during and after the war. If there is a great war in 2001 and it is not catastrophic (a real possibility), the crimes of that war will be revisited upon the US over the next generation. That is not some kind of religious prophecy or threat, it is merely a straightforward political analysis.

"Enslave your girls and women, harbor anti-US terrorists, destroy every vestige of civilization in your homeland, and the Bush administration will embrace you. All that matters is that you line up as an ally in the drug war, the only international cause that this nation still takes seriously. That's the message sent with the recent gift of $43 million to the Taliban rulers of Afghanistan, the most virulent anti-American violators of human rights in the world today. "

– Robert Scheer, *Los Angeles Times*, May 22, 2001

THE "SECURITY" CHARADE
Bishop Robert Bowman

[Ed's note: Robert Bowman flew 101 combat missions in Vietnam. He is presently (since 1998) bishop of the United Catholic Church in Melbourne Beach, FL. Originally printed in *The National Catholic Reporter*, Oct. 2, 1998.]

If deceptions about terrorism go unchallenged, then the threat will continue until it destroys us.

The truth is that none of our thousands of nuclear weapons can protect us from these threats. No Star Wars system no matter how technically advanced, no matter how many trillions of dollars are poured into it, can protect us from a nuclear weapon delivered in a sailboat or a Cessna or a suitcase or a Ryder rental truck. Not one weapon in our vast arsenal, not a penny of the $270 billion a year we spend on so-called defense can defend against a terrorist bomb. That is a military fact.

"We're caught between bin Laden who's a violent Islamic religious fanatic and Bush who's a violent Christian religious fanatic. And we're caught in the middle."

- Ras Baraka

As a retired lieutenant colonel and a frequent lecturer on national security issues, I have often quoted Psalm 33: "A king is not saved by his mighty army. A warrior is not saved by his great strength." The obvious reaction is, "Then what can we do?" Is there nothing we can do to provide security for our people?"

There is. But to understand it requires that we know the truth about the threat. President Clinton did not tell the American people the truth about why we are the targets of terrorism when he explained why we bombed Afghanistan and Sudan. He said that we are a target because we stand for democracy, freedom, and human rights in the world. Nonsense!

We are the target of terrorists because, in much of the world, our government stands for dictatorship, bondage, and human exploitation. We are the target of terrorists because we are hated. And we are hated because our government has done hateful things. In country after country, our government has thwarted democracy, stifled freedom, and trampled human rights. That's why it is hated around the world. And that's why we're the target of terrorists.

People in Canada enjoy democracy, freedom, and human rights. So do the people of Norway and Sweden. Have you heard of Canadian embassies being bombed? Or Norwegian, or Swedish?

We are not hated because we practice democracy, value freedom, or uphold human rights. We are hated because our government denies these things to people in Third World countries whose resources are coveted by our multinational corporations. That hatred we have sown has come back to haunt us in the form of terrorism and in the future, nuclear terrorism.

Once the truth about why the threat exists is understood, the solution becomes obvious. We must change our ways. Getting rid of our nuclear weapons unilaterally if necessary will enhance our security. Drastically altering our foreign policy will ensure it.

Instead of sending our sons and daughters around the world to kill Arabs so we can have the oil under their sand, we should send them to rebuild their infrastructure, supply clean water, and feed starving children. Instead of continuing to kill hundreds of Iraqi children every day with our sanctions, we should help Iraqis rebuild their electric power plants, their water treatment facilities, their hospitals, and all the things we have destroyed and prevented them from rebuilding.

77

Instead of training terrorists and death squads, we should close the School of the Americas (Ft. Benning, GA.). Instead of supporting insurrection, destabilization, assassination, and terror around the world, we should abolish the CIA and give money to relief agencies.

In short, we should do good instead of evil. Who would try to stop us? Who would hate us? Who would want to bomb us? That is the truth the American people need to hear. We need to "respond" NOT "react."

God Bless
Bishop Bowman

"Injustice is the most eloquent recruiter for terrorism."
- John Maxwell

THE THEATRE OF GOOD AND EVIL

Eduardo Galeano, Translated by Justin Podur

In the struggle of Good against Evil, it's always the people who get killed. The terrorists killed workers of 50 countries in NYC and DC, in the name of Good against Evil. And in the name of Good against Evil President Bush has promised vengeance: "We will eliminate Evil from the world," he announced. Eliminate Evil? What would Good be without Evil? It's not just religious fanatics who need enemies to justify their insanity. The arms industry and the gigantic war machine of the US also needs enemies to justify its existence. Good and evil, evil and good: the actors change masks, the heroes become monsters and the monsters heroes, in accord with the demands of the theatre's playwrights. This is nothing new. The German scientist Werner von Braun was evil when he invented the V-2 bombers that Hitler used against London, but became good when he used his talents in the service of the US. Stalin was good during World War Two and evil afterwards, when he became the leader of the Evil Empire. In the cold war years John Steinbeck wrote: "Maybe the whole world needs Russians. I suppose that even in Russia they need Russians. Maybe Russia's Russians are called Americans." Even the Russians became good afterwards.

Accurate scholarship can
Unearth the whole offence
From Luther until now
That has driven a culture mad,
Find what occurred at Linz,
What huge imago made
A psychopathic god:
I and the public know
What all schoolchildren learn,
Those to whom evil is done
Do evil in return.

- W. H. Auden, "September 1, 1939"

Today, Putin can add his voice to say: "Evil must be punished." Saddam Hussein was good, and so were the chemical weapons he used against the Iranians and the Kurds. Afterwards, he became evil. They were calling him Satan Hussein when the US finished up their invasion of Panama to invade Iraq because Iraq invaded Kuwait. Father Bush that particular war against Evil upon himself. With the humanitarian and compassionate spirit that characterizes his family, he killed more than 100,000 Iraqis, the vast majority of them civilians. Satan Hussein stayed where he was, but this number one enemy of humanity had to step aside and

accept becoming number two enemy of humanity. The bane of the world is now
called Osama bin Laden. The CIA taught him everything he knows about
terrorism: bin Laden, loved and armed by the US government, was one of the
principal 'freedom fighters' against Communism in Afghanistan. Father Bush
occupied the Vice Presidency when President Reagan called these heroes 'the
moral equivalents of the Founding Fathers.' Hollywood agreed.

They filmed *Rambo 3*: Afghani Muslims were the good guys. Now, 13 years
later, in the time of Son Bush, they are the worst of the bad guys. Henry
Kissinger was one of the first to react to the recent tragedy. "Those who
provide support, financing, and inspiration to terrorists are as guilty as the
terrorists themselves," he intoned, words that Son Bush would repeat hours
later. If that's how it is, the urgent need right now is to bomb Kissinger. He is
guilty of many more crimes than bin Laden or any terrorist in the world. And in
many more countries. He provided 'support, financing, and inspiration" to state
terror in Indonesia, Cambodia, Iran, South Africa, Bangladesh, and all the South
American countries that suffered the dirty war of Plan Condor. On September
11 1973, exactly 28 years before the fires of last week, the Presidential Palace
in Chile was stormed. Kissinger had written the epitaph of Allende and Chilean
democracy long before when he commented on the results of the elections: "I
don't see why we have to stand by and watch a country go communist because
of the irresponsibility of its own people." A contempt for the people is one of
many things shared by state and private terror. For example, the ETA, an
organization that kills people in the name of independence in Basque Country,
says through one of its spokespeople: 'Rights have nothing to do with
majorities or minorities.'

There is much common ground between low- and high- tech terrorism, between
the terrorism of religious fanatics and that of market fanatics, that of the
hopeless and that of the powerful, that of the psychopath on the loose and that
of the cold-blooded uniformed professional. They all share the disrespect for
human life: the killers of the 5500 citizens under the Twin Towers that fell like
castles of dry sand– and the killers of 200 000 Guatemalans, the majority of
whom were indigenous, exterminated without television or the newspapers of
the world paying any attention. Those Guatemalans were not sacrificed by any
Muslim fanatic, but by terrorist squads who received 'support, financing, and
inspiration' from successive US governments. All these worshipers of death are
in agreement as well on the need to reduce social, cultural, and national
differences to military terms. In the name of Good against Evil, in the name of
the One Truth, they resolve everything by killing first and asking questions later.
And by this method, they strengthen the enemy they fight. It was the atrocities
of the Sendero Luminoso that gave President Fujimori the popular support he

sought to unleash a regime of terror and sell Peru for the price of a banana. It was the atrocities of the US in the Middle East that prepared the ground for the holy war of terrorism of Allah. Although the leader of the Civilized World is pushing a new Crusade, Allah is innocent of the crimes committed in his name. At the end of the day, God did not order the Holocaust against the followers of Jehovah, nor did Jehovah order the massacres of Sabrah and Shatila or the expulsion of Palestinians from their land. Aren't Allah, God and Jehovah are, after all, three names for the same divinity?

A tragedy of errors: nobody knows any more who is who. The smoke of the explosions forms part of the much larger curtain of smoke that prevents all of us from seeing clearly. From revenge to revenge, terrorism obliges us to walk to our graves. I saw a photo, recently published, of graffiti on a wall in NYC: "An eye for an eye makes the whole world blind." The spiral of violence creates violence and also confusion: pain, fear, intolerance, hatred, insanity. In Porto Alegre, at the beginning of this year, Ahmed Ben Bella warned: 'This system, that has already made mad cows, is making mad people too." And these mad people, mad from hate, act as the power that created them. A three year old child, named Luca, told me: "The world doesn't know where its house is." He was looking at a map. He could have been looking at a reporter.

"It's really not a number I'm terribly interested in. "
- General Colin Powell (When asked about the Iraqi s killed in 1991's "Desert Storm")

According to the United Nations Food and Agriculture Organization (FAO), about 35,615 children died from conditions of starvation on September 11, 2001.

Relevant Statistics:

Victims: 35,615 children
Where: poor countries
Special TV programs: none
Newspaper articles: none
Messages from the president: none
Solidarity acts: none
Minutes of silence: none
Victims mournings: none
Organized forums: none
Pope messages: none
Alert level: zero
Military mobilization: none

The American people may be a little fuzzy about where exactly Afghanistan is, but the US government and Afghanistan are old friends. In 1979, after the Soviet invasion of Afghanistan, the CIA and Pakistan's ISI (Inter Services Intelligence) launched the largest covert operation in the history of the CIA. Their purpose was to harness the energy of Afghan resistance to the Soviets and expand it into a holy war, an Islamic jihad, which would turn Muslim countries within the Soviet Union against the communist regime and eventually destabilise it. When it began, it was meant to be the Soviet Union's Vietnam. It turned out to be much more than that. Over the years, through the ISI, the CIA funded and recruited almost 100,000 radical mojahedin from 40 Islamic countries as soldiers for America's proxy war. The rank and file of the mojahedin were unaware that their jihad was actually being fought on behalf of Uncle Sam. (The irony is that America was equally unaware that it was financing a future war against itself.) In 1989, after being bloodied by 10 years of relentless conflict, the Russians withdrew, leaving behind a civilisation reduced to rubble. Civil war in Afghanistan raged on.

The jihad spread to Chechnya, Kosovo and eventually to Kashmir. The CIA continued to pour in money and military equipment, but the overheads had become immense, and more money was needed. The mojahedin ordered farmers to plant opium as a "revolutionary tax". The ISI set up hundreds of heroin laboratories across Afghanistan. Within two years of the CIA's arrival, the Pakistan-Afghanistan borderland had become the biggest producer of heroin in the world, and the single biggest source of the heroin on American streets. The annual profits, said to be between $100bn and $200bn, were ploughed back into training and arming militants. In 1995, the Taliban - then a marginal sect of dangerous, hardline fundamentalists - fought its way to power in Afghanistan. It was funded by the ISI, that old cohort of the CIA, and supported by many political parties in Pakistan. The Taliban unleashed a regime of terror. Its first victims were its own people, particularly women. It closed down girls' schools, dismissed women from government jobs, and enforced sharia laws under which women deemed to be "immoral" are stoned to death, and widows guilty of being adulterous are buried alive. Given the Taliban government's human rights track record, it seems unlikely that it will in any way be intimidated or swerved from its purpose by the prospect of war, or the threat to the lives of its civilians. After all that has happened, can there be anything more ironic than Russia and America joining hands to re-destroy Afghanistan?

- Arundhati Roy

"The greatest crime since World War II has been US foreign policy."
- Ramsey Clark (Former US Attorney General under President Lyndon Johnson)

UNNECESSARY EVILS

© Jan Blankenstein/Stichting Amsterdam Photo Art 2001

"I will never apologize for the United States of America – I don't care what the facts are."

- President George Bush, 1988 (On the shooting down of an Iranian commercial airliner on July 3, 1988 by the US Navy warship Vincennes. All 290 civilian people in the aircraft were killed. The plane was on a routine flight in a commercial corridor in Iranian airspace.)

MAKE NO MISTAKE
Ted Rall, AlterNet
October 11, 2001

Nursultan Nazarbayev has a terrible problem. He's the president and former Communist Party boss of Kazakhstan, the second-largest republic of the former Soviet Union. A few years ago, the giant country struck oil in the eastern portion of the Caspian Sea. Geologists estimate that sitting beneath the wind-blown steppes of Kazakhstan are 50 billion barrels of oil – by far the biggest untapped reserves in the world. (Saudi Arabia, currently the world's largest oil producer, is believed to have about 30 billion barrels remaining.)

Kazakhstan's Soviet-subsidized economy collapsed immediately after independence in 1991.

Nazarbayev has spent most of the last decade trying to get his land-locked oil out to sea. Once the oil starts flowing, it won't take long before Kazakhstan replaces Kuwait as the land of Benzes and ugly gold jewelry. But the longer the pipeline, the more expensive and vulnerable to sabotage it is. The shortest

```
To: Jeremy Glick
From: Jee Kim
Subject: Speaking of nicks

Whatever happened to that cop that shot that black kid
sparking riots in Cincinnati right before all this?

That cop is happy as hell right now, all the attention
is off him. And a lot of other folks are smiling right
now too. Israel catching wreck on Palestine? They're
smiling. Security businesses and their shareholders are
smiling.

A lot of shit is being slid right under our noses; I
feel like we're being told a "fairy tale for children,"
lulled asleep while our government goes out to indulge
in unnecessary evils. Look at all the shit that has
already gone down in environment, civil rights, funding,
and appointees. (someone sent me this great email, look
below)
one
```

The First Six Months of George W. Bush:
Whatever your beliefs, know what your president is doing. Here is a list of his work in his first six months:

— Significantly eased field-testing controls of genetically engineered crops.
— Cut federal spending on libraries by $39 million.
— Cut $35 million in funding for doctors to get advanced pediatric training.
— Cut by 50% funding for research into renewable energy sources.

route runs through Iran, but Kazakhstan is too closely aligned with the US to offend it by cutting a deal with Teheran. Russia has helpfully offered to build a line connecting Kazakh oil rigs to the Black Sea, but neighboring Turkmenistan has experienced trouble with the Russians: they tend to divert the oil for their own uses without paying for it. There's even a plan to run crude out through China, but the proposed 5,300-mile line would be far too long to prove profitable.

The logical alternative, then, is Unocal's plan, which is to extend Turkmenistan's existing system west to the Kazakh field on the Caspian and southeast to the Pakistani port of Karachi on the Arabian Sea. That project runs through Afghanistan.

As Central Asian expert Ahmed Rashid describes in his 2000 book *Taliban: Militant Islam, Oil and Fundamentalism in Central Asia*, the US and Pakistan decided to install a stable regime in Afghanistan around 1994 – a regime that would end the country's civil war and thus ensure the safety of the Unocal pipeline project. Impressed by the ruthlessness and willingness of the then-emerging Taliban to cut a pipeline deal, the US State Department and Pakistan's ISI intelligence service agreed to funnel arms and funding to the Taliban in their war against the ethnically Tajik Northern Alliance. As recently as 1999, US taxpayers paid the entire annual salary of every single Taliban government official, all in the hopes of returning to the days of dollar-a-gallon gas. Pakistan, naturally, would pick up revenues from a Karachi oil port facility. Harkening to 19th century power politics between Russia and British India, Rashid dubbed the struggle for control of post-Soviet Central Asia "the new Great Game."

85

Predictably, the Taliban Frankenstein got out of control. The regime's unholy alliance with Osama bin Laden's terror network, their penchant for invading their neighbors and their production of 50 percent of the world's opium made them unlikely partners for the desired oil deal.

"We must become the owners, or at any rate the controllers at the source, of at least a proportion of the oil which we require."
- British Royal Commission, 1913 (agreeing with Winston Churchill's policy towards Iraq)

— Revoked rules that reduced the acceptable levels of arsenic in drinking water.
— Blocked rules that would require federal agencies to offer bilingual assistance to non-English speaking persons. This, from a candidate who would readily fire-up his Spanish-speaking skills in front of would-be Hispanic voters.
— Proposed to eliminate new marine protections for the Channel Islands and the coral reefs of northwest Hawaii. San Francisco Chronicle, April 6, 2001

Finally the Bushies had the perfect excuse to do what the US had wanted all along: invade and/or install an old-school puppet regime in Kabul. Realpolitik no more cares about the 6,000 dead than it concerns itself with oppressed women in Afghanistan; this ersatz war by a phony president is solely about getting the Unocal deal done without interference from annoying local middlemen.

As Bush would say, make no mistake: this is about oil. It's always about oil. And to twist a late '90s cliché, it's only boring because it's true.

STATEMENT OF JOHN J. MARESCA
Vice President of International Relations, Unocal Corporation

US Interests in the Central Asian Republics Hearing before the Subcommittee on Asia and the Pacific of the Committee on International Relations. House of Representatives, 150th Congress, 2nd Session, February 12, 1998

Unocal, as you know, is one of the world's leading energy resource and project development companies... I congratulate you for focusing on Central Asia oil and gas reserves and the role they play in shaping US policy.

Mr. Chairman, the Caspian region contains tremendous untapped hydrocarbon reserves. Just to give an idea of the scale, proven natural gas reserves equal more than 236 trillion cubic feet. The region's total oil reserves may well reach more than 60 billion barrels of oil. Some estimates are as high as 200 billion barrels.

One major problem has yet to be resolved: how to get the region's vast energy resources to the markets where they are needed. Central Asia is isolated. Their natural resources are landlocked, both geographically and politically. Each of the countries in the Caucasus and Central Asia faces difficult political challenges. Some have unsettled wars or latent conflicts. Others have evolving systems where the laws and even the courts are dynamic and changing. In addition, a chief technical obstacle which we in the industry face in transporting oil is the region's existing pipeline infrastructure...

— Cut funding by 28% for research into cleaner, more efficient cars and trucks.
— Suspended rules that would have strengthened the government's ability to deny contracts to companies that violated workplace safety, environmental and other federal laws.
— OK'd Interior Department appointee Gale Norton to send out letters to state officials soliciting suggestions for opening up national monuments for oil and gas drilling, coal mining, and foresting.
— Appointed John Negroponte, an un-indicted high level Iran Contra figure, to the post of United Nations ambassador.

...The key question then is how the energy resources of Central Asia can be made available to nearby Asian markets. There are two possible solutions, with several variations. One option is to go east across China, but this would mean constructing a pipeline of more than 3,000 kilometers just to reach Central China. In addition, there would have to be a 2,000 kilometer connection to reach the main population centers along the coast. The question then is what will be the cost of transporting oil through this pipeline, and what would be the netback which the producers would receive...

"If they turn on the radars we're going to blow up their goddamn SAMs (surface-to-air missiles). They know we own their country. We own their airspace... We dictate the way they live and talk. And that's what's great about America right now. It's a good thing, especially when there's a lot of oil out there we need."

87

- US Brig. General William Looney (Referring to the mass-murder of hundreds of civilian Iraqi men, women and children during 10,000 sorties by American/British forces in the first eight months of 1999)

The second option is to build a pipeline south from Central Asia to the Indian Ocean. One obvious route south would cross Iran, but this is foreclosed for American companies because of US sanctions legislation. The only other possible route is across Afghanistan, which has of course its own unique challenges. The country has been involved in bitter warfare for almost two decades, and is still divided by civil war. From the outset, we have made it clear that construction of the pipeline we have proposed across Afghanistan could not begin until a recognized government is in place that has the confidence of governments, lenders, and our company...

— Abandoned a campaign pledge to invest $100 million for rain forest conservation.
— Reduced by 86% the Community Access Program for public hospitals, clinics and providers of care for people without insurance.
— Rescinded a proposal to increase public access to information about the potential consequences resulting from chemical plant accidents.
— Suspended rules that would require hardrock miners to clean up sites on Western public lands.

NEGROPONTE IS THE WRONG U.S. MESSENGER

Frank del Olmo, *Los Angeles Times*

In the wake of all the media coverage of the terrorist attacks on the East Coast, one news story got very little attention: the Senate's Sept. 14 approval of John Negroponte to be the US ambassador to United Nations. The timing could not have been worse, given President Bush's by-then urgent campaign to rally international opinion against terrorism and the thugs who carry it out. Negroponte's nomination, which had been held up for half a year because of his record on human rights, was ramrodded through the Senate Foreign Relations Committee on Sept. 13 on a 14-3 vote. The next day, the Senate approved it as a routine consent item, i.e., without even a formal floor vote.

"The first victims of whatever military actions are undertaken will be the billions of people living in the poor and underdeveloped world with their unbelievable economic and social problems, their unpayable debts and the ruinous prices of their basic commodities, their growing natural and ecological catastrophes, their hunger and misery, the massive undernourishment of their children, teenagers and adults, their terrible AIDS epidemic, their malaria, their tuberculosis, and their infectious diseases that threaten whole nations with extermination."

- Fidel Castro, September 22, 2001

We may yet come to realize how far from routine the Negroponte nomination was. For as nations all over the world close ranks with the US in its new war against terrorism, the comparative silence south of the border has been deafening. Sure, most Latin America governments have expressed regret over the loss of life in the immediate aftermath of the terrorist attacks, but there has been no substantial show of solidarity by any Latin American leader since

---

— Cut $60 million from a Boy's and Girl's Clubs of America program for public housing.
— Proposed to eliminate a federal program designed to help communities (and successfully used in Seattle) prepare for natural disasters.
— Pulled out of the 1997 Kyoto Treaty global warming agreement.
— Cut $200 million of work force training for dislocated workers.
— Proposes that $1.2 billion in funding for alternative renewable energy come from selling oil and gas lease tracts in the Alaska National Wildlife Reserve.

```
To: Jee Kim
From: Jeremy Glick
Subject: other evils

Don't forget all the Afghanis that are dying, without a
single thought.

Btw, Look what just came out, with no media attention,
the cop in Cincinnati… A judge acquitted the cop that
killed that unarmed brother. From one of the papers:
"Hamilton County Municipal Court Judge Ted Winkler,
deciding the case without a jury, ruled that Stephen
Roach, 27, was justified in the shooting of Timothy
Thomas, who the officer said he chased into a dark alley
and shot when Thomas ignored orders to 'show his hands'
and appeared to go for a gun."

The cop didn't even testify during the trial! And he got
acquitted of the lesser charges of "obstructing official
business," which he was charged with for differing
accounts of the shooting.

With all this cop love going around, everyone has
forgotten shit like this.
```

89

then, with the exception of Mexico's President Vicente Fox. It would be a mistake to assume that this is just another case of knee-jerk anti-gringo feelings in Latin America or to expect our southern neighbors to eventually come around. For by putting Negroponte in a key foreign policy post, Bush has rewarded a US diplomat whom many Latin Americans consider a terrorist–albeit of the well-bred, Ivy League variety.

Negroponte is a career foreign service officer whose first ambassadorial post was in Honduras in 1981-85 when Central America was one of the hot fronts in the Cold War. There, he was paymaster for an unsavory covert army known as the Contras, who, under the tutelage of the US, waged a dirty little war against the Sandinista government in Nicaragua. To give the Contras a free hand to operate from Honduran territory, Negroponte purchased the cooperation of the corrupt generals who ran Honduras at the time, underwriting a death squad they used against political opponents, according to documents the Senate Foreign Relations Committee had before it. Several investigations have documented the activities of that death squad, known as Battalion 316. It was funded and even

— Eliminated funding for the Wetlands Reserve Program, which encourages farmers to maintain wetlands habitat on their property.
— Cut program to provide childcare to low-income families as they move from welfare to work.
— Cut a program that provided prescription contraceptive coverage to federal employees (though it still pays for Viagra).
— Cut $700 million in capital funds for repairs in public housing.

© Jan Blankenstein/Stichting Amsterdam Photo Art 2001

partly trained by the CIA. And recently declassified CIA and State Department documents indicate that Negroponte knew more about that death squad's operations than he reported to Congress at the time, as the law required him to do.

During the pro forma committee meeting Sept. 13, Negroponte claimed his reports and judgments about the Honduran military "were made in good faith." Pretty lame words considering the enormity of what Battalion 316 did to its fellow Hondurans. It is no exaggeration to say that Battalion 316's dirty work induced the same kind of terror in a small nation of 6million people that the recent bloodshed in New York City, Washington and Pennsylvania did in this country. Among Battalion 316's victims were 184 Hondurans and at least one US citizen, a Jesuit priest named Joseph Carney.

Little wonder, then, that Latin Americans think Negroponte has blood on his hands as surely as Osama bin Laden has blood on his. Bush, not to mention Negroponte's good friend, Secretary of State Colin Powell, should have realized how hypocritical it would look for us to apply one set of moral standards to terrorists who killed thousands of innocent people in a few terrible hours while at the same time we use another set to judge a man who oversaw American aid to military thugs who did similarly cruel things to Central Americans. Even assuming, for a moment, that morality doesn't matter in international affairs, especially during wartime, what about pragmatism? Can Negroponte be the effective voice we will need at the UN the next few years? Not very likely. Oh, the new US ambassador will get the UN's attention when he speaks up. He represents a superpower, after all. But if and when Negroponte has the gall to lecture the world about human rights, no one could blame UN diplomats for holding their noses. The stench of hypocrisy will be that bad.

— Appointed Otto Reich, an un-indicted high level Iran Contra figure, to Assistant Secretary of State for Inter-American Affairs.
— Cut Environmental Protection Agency budget by $500 million.
— Proposed to curtail the ability of groups to sue in order to get an animal placed on the Endangered Species List.
— Rescinded rule that mandated increased energy-saving efficiency regulations for central air conditioners and heat pumps.

WHEN JOURNALISTS REPORT FOR DUTY
Norman Solomon

In *Time* magazine's special issue about the events of Sept. 11, chilling photos evoke the horrific slaughter in Manhattan. All of the pages are deadly serious. And on the last page, under the headline "The Case for Rage and Retribution," an essay by *Time* regular Lance Morrow declares: "A day cannot live in infamy without the nourishment of rage. Let's have rage." Exhorting our country to relearn the lost virtues of "self-confident relentlessness" and "hatred," the article calls for "a policy of focused brutality." It's an apt conclusion to an edition of the nation's biggest news magazine that embodies the human strengths and ominous defects of American media during the current crisis. Much of the initial news coverage was poignant, grief-stricken and utterly appropriate. But many news analysts and pundits lost no time conveying – sometimes with great enthusiasm – their eagerness to see the United States use its military might in anger. Such impulses are extremely dangerous.

91

For instance, night after night on cable television, Bill O'Reilly has been banging his loud drum for indiscriminate reprisals. Unless the Taliban quickly hands over Osama bin Laden, he proclaimed on Fox News Channel, "the US should bomb the Afghan infrastructure to rubble – the airport, the power plants, their water facilities and the roads. "What about the civilian population of Afghanistan? "We should not target civilians," O'Reilly said, "but if they don't rise up against this criminal government, they starve, period."

"Israel has been clear in its intention to take every advantage of the terrorist attacks in the US. In only the first three days after the New York/Washington attacks, gloated Israeli Defense Minister Binyamin Ben Eliezer, 'we have killed 14 Palestinians in Jenin, Kabatyeh and Tammun, with the world remaining absolutely silent.'"

- Phyllis Bennis

— Repealed workplace ergonomic rules designed to improve worker health and safety.
— Abandoned campaign pledge to regulate carbon dioxide (CO_2), the waste gas that contributes to global warming.
— Banned federal aid to international family planning programs that offer abortion counseling with other independent funds.
— Closed White House Office for Women's Health Initiatives and Outreach.

6. today it is ten days. last night bush waged war on a man once

openly funded by the cia. i do not know who is responsible. read too many

books, know

too many people to believe what i am told. i don't give a fuck about

bin laden. his vision of the world does not include me or those i

love. and petitions have been going around for years trying to get

the US sponsored taliban out of power. shit is complicated, and i

don't know what to think.

but i know for sure who will pay.

in the world, it will be women, mostly colored and poor. women will

have to bury children, and support themselves through grief. "either

you are with us, or with the terrorists" - meaning keep your people

under control and your resistance censored. meaning we got the loot

and the nukes.

– Suheir Hammad, "First Writing Since"

92

THE WARTIME OPPORTUNISTS
Russell Mokhiber and Robert Weissman

Make way for the wartime opportunists.

Corporate interests and their proxies are looking to exploit the September 11 tragedy to advance a self-serving agenda that has nothing to do with national security and everything to do with corporate profits and dangerous ideologies.

Fast track and the Free Trade Area of the Americas. A corporate tax cut. Oil

— Nominated David Lauriski, ex-mining company executive, to post of Assistant Secretary of Labor for Mine Safety and Health.
— O.K.'d Interior Secretary Gale Norton to go forth with a controversial plan to auction oil and gas development tracts off the eastern coast of Florida.
— Announced intention to open up Montana's Lewis and Clark National Forest to oil and drilling.
— Proposes to re-draw boundaries of nation's monuments, which would technically allow oil and gas drilling "outside" of national monuments.

drilling in Alaska. Star Wars. These are some of the preposterous "solutions" and responses to the terror attack offered by corporate mouthpieces. No one has been more shameless in linking their agenda to the terror attack than US Trade Representative Robert Zoellick. Writing in the Washington Post last week, Zoellick proclaimed that granting fast-track trade negotiating authority to the president – to assist with the ramming through Congress of a Free Trade Area of the Americas, designed to expand NAFTA to all of the Americas, among other nefarious ends – was the best way to respond to the September 11 tragedy. "Earlier enemies learned that America is the arsenal of democracy," Zoellick wrote, "Today's enemies will learn that America is the economic engine for freedom, opportunity and development. To that end, US leadership in promoting the international economic and trading system is vital. Trade is about more than economic efficiency. It promotes the values at the heart of this protracted struggle." No explanation from Zoellick about how adopting a procedural rule designed to limit Congressional debate on controversial trade agreements advances the democratic and rule-of-law values he says the United States must now project. The administration has identified fast track as one of the handful of legislative priorities it hopes to see Congress enact this year. Getting fast track passed isn't big business's only priority for the shrinking legislative calendar.

93

The Fortune 500 has been whimpering since George Bush was elected president and top administration officials told the business community to silence their demand for corporate tax cuts until after passage of the inequality-increasing personal income tax cut. Even before the September 11 attack, business interests and the anti-tax ideologues were increasingly making noise that corporate tax cuts were the solution to the coming recession. Now they are beginning to argue that capital gains tax cuts and corporate tax breaks are America's patriotic duty. In releasing a study purporting to explain how a capital gains cut would encourage economic growth, the National Taxpayers Union (NTU) touted a capital gains tax cut – a tax break that exclusively benefits the wealthy — as an anti-terrorism initiative. "By reducing the rate at which capital gains are taxed, President Bush and Congress could help revitalize the sagging economy and bring new revenues to Washington – decidedly aiding our war against terrorism," said NTU director of congressional relations Eric Schlecht.

— Gutted White House AIDS Office.

— Renegotiating free trade agreement with Jordan to eliminate safeguards for the environment and workers' rights.

— Will no longer seek guidance from The American Bar Association in recommendations for the federal judiciary appointments.

— Appointed recycling foe Lynn Scarlett as Undersecretary of the Interior.

Not wishing to be outdone, Senator Frank Murkowski, R-Alaska, didn't wait long to explain how the terror attack makes it imperative to open up the Arctic National Wildlife Refuge (ANWR). "There is no doubt that at this time of national emergency, an expedited energy-security bill must be considered," the Alaska senator announced last week. "Opening ANWR will be a central element in finally reducing this country's dangerous overdependence on unstable foreign sources of energy," he said.

Neither Murkowski nor the oil companies pushing for opening ANWR have ever been able to offer a coherent explanation of how using up US oil reserves heightens energy security. Security rests in maintaining the reserves. Real energy security and independence can only come from renewables (particularly solar and wind) – where the supply is plentiful and infinitely renewing. Only a failure of public and private investment leaves the country (and the world) unable to harvest renewable energy efficiently.

And, of course, the purveyors of Star Wars couldn't let the opportunity pass them by. The Center for Security Policy –the center of a web of defense industry-backed think tanks and organizations pushing for a National Missile Defense program – urged President Bush in advance of his address to Congress to announce that "this Administration will use every tool at its disposal to ensure that the resources and latitude needed to develop and deploy missile defenses are made available."

© Richard Yeh 2001

— Took steps to abolish the White House Council on Environmental Quality.
— Cut the Community Oriented Policing Services program.
— Allowed Interior Secretary Gale Norton to shelve citizen-led grizzly bear re-introduction plan scheduled for Idaho and Montana wilderness.
— Makes sure convicted misdemeanor drug users cannot get financial aid for college, though convicted murderers can.

BUSH'S WAR ON TERRORISM: WHO WILL PAY AND WHO WILL BENEFIT?

William Hartung

In the first few days after the attacks on the Pentagon and the World Trade Center, President Bush had already described them as acts of war, setting the stage for the introduction of a new "war on terrorism." Congress quickly approved a $40 billion emergency funding package, to be divided equally between domestic reconstruction efforts and support for federal agencies that will be engaged in the fight against terrorism.

Picking up on a theme that had been sounded earlier by Deputy Secretary of Defense Paul Wolfowitz, the President asserted before a joint session of Congress on September 20th that the administration's war on terrorism would be a multi-faceted, long-term effort encompassing covert actions, military strikes, diplomatic initiatives, and domestic security measures (underscored by his creation of a Cabinet-level Department of Homeland Defense, to be headed by Pennsylvania Governor Tom Ridge). The speech was long on resolve and short on details on the costs and consequences of this seemingly open-ended anti-terror campaign.

95

A BLANK CHECK FOR THE PENTAGON?

Although there has been considerable editorial comment about the need to rethink US defense strategy in the wake of the September 11th attacks, so far it appears to be business as usual. An article in the September 17-23 issue of *Defense News* indicates that roughly $12 billion of the $40 billion emergency package is slated to go to the Pentagon, but it quotes a Pentagon official as saying that the emergency funds "will have nothing to do with rescue and emergency efforts." The official further states that "This will have nothing to do with retaliation in response to the Sept. 11 attacks. The funding will go to the [military department's] wish lists for things that we'll have several years from now." Budget analyst Christopher Hellman of the Center for Defense Information has suggested that military spending for the fiscal year starting October 1, 2001 could reach $375 billion. Deputy Secretary of Defense Wolfowitz has intimated that the emergency funds are just the down payment on a major

— Refused to fund continued cleanup of uranium-slag heap in Utah.
— Refused to fund continued litigation of the government's tobacco company lawsuit.
— Proposed a $2 trillion tax cut, of which 43% will go to the wealthiest 1% of Americans.
— Signed a bill making it harder for poor and middle-class Americans to file for bankruptcy, even in the case of daunting medical bills.

increase in Pentagon spending, and conservative analysts such as Loren
Thompson of the Lexington Institute have suggested that it is possible that
Congress will now be willing to push the Pentagon budget to $400 billion per
year or more, a figure that was merely a right-wing pipe dream just a few
months ago.

This surge in Pentagon spending is good news for major Pentagon contractors,
who were among the few companies that showed increases in their stock prices
when the market reopened after the September 11th attacks. Among the top
gainers for the week of September 17-21 were major military and space
contractors like Raytheon (+37%), L-3 Communications (+35.8%), EDO
(+24.8%), Alliant Tech Systems (+23.5%), and Northrop Grumman (+21.2%). As
James Dao of the *New York Times* noted, some companies are already up on
Capitol Hill pushing their wares in the wake of the September 11th attacks:
"Many military contractors have been hesitant to talk publicly about their
improved economic prospects. 'This is such a gruesome way to make money,' a
lobbyist said." But other companies, like Continental Electronics, have begun
openly lobbying for new business, going so far as to call the Pentagon directly.
"We believe that our radio transmitters would be desperately needed in places
like Pakistan," said John Uvodich, the company's president. "We are just trying
to let people in Washington know that we are here to assist."

A logical approach to retooling the Pentagon would be to set some priorities,
not just throw money at the problem under the guise of fighting terrorism.
Systems like the costly F-22 fighter plane, the bulky Crusader artillery system,
and the administration's $8.3 billion missile defense program seem largely
irrelevant to dealing with low tech threats like the September 11th attacks. But
as Joseph Cirincione of the Carnegie Endowment for International Peace notes,
"tragically, some are using the terrible tragedy to justify their existing programs,
slapping an 'anti-terrorism' label on missile defense and military budget

96

— Appointed a Vice President quoted as saying, "If you want to do something about carbon
  dioxide emissions, then you ought to build nuclear power plants." (Vice President Dick Cheney
  on "Meet the Press.")
— Appointed Diana "There is no gender gap in pay" Roth to the Council of Economic Advisers.
  Boston Globe, March 28, 2001
— Appointed Kay Cole James, an opponent of affirmative action, to direct the Office of
  Personnel Management.
— Cut $15.7 million earmarked for states to investigate cases of child abuse and neglect.

increases." Just as no one in the Bush administration has adequately explained why the expect a military response to terrorism to be effective, no one has indicated why a $375 billion budget – comparable to what the US was spending during the Cold War against an adversary with 4 million troops and thousands of nuclear weapons – is not sufficient to fight a series of terrorist networks whose membership is measured in the thousands, not the millions.

BY THE WAY, ABOUT THAT MISSILE DEFENSE SYSTEM

Despite the fact that a number of informed observers, including Senate Foreign Relations Committee Chairman Joseph Biden of Delaware, have noted that the September 11th attacks underscore the irrelevance of the Bush administration's costly missile defense scheme to the most immediate threats to US security, the program may receive a short-term boost in the environment of "consensus" that now reigns on Capitol Hill. A few days after the attacks, The *New York Times* reported that key Capitol Hill Democrats did not want to appear to be partisan by picking a fight on missile defense at this time. But as Tom Collina of the Union of Concerned Scientists aptly noted, "There's a real danger because of this crisis that the Democrats will give up this fight, which would be a real shame." Armed Services Committee Chairman Carl Levin agreed to hold off on an amendment that would have limited the ability of the administration to undertake tests or other actions that would violate the Anti-Ballistic Missile Treaty. He promises to introduce the measure later as a stand-alone measure.

In the mean time, Star Wars boosters are using homey analogies to suggest that we need anti-terrorist measures and missile defense, saying things like "just because the burglar came in the front door last time doesn't mean you want to leave the back door unlocked," or "just because you have insurance against theft doesn't mean you shouldn't buy fire insurance." These comparisons are way off the mark. Given the extreme unlikelihood of a nuclear-armed state, much less a terrorist group, launching a nuclear missile attack at the United States, a more accurate analogy would be more like "Now that your house has just burned down, maybe you should stop spending all your money on insurance against being hit by an asteroid."

— Helped kill a law designed to make it tougher for teenagers to get credit cards.
— Proposed elimination of the "Reading is Fundamental" program that gives free books to poor children.
— Is pushing for development of small nuclear weapons to attack deeply buried targets-weapons, which would violate the Comprehensive Test Ban Treaty.
— Proposes to nominate Jeffrey Sutton, attorney responsible for the recent case weakening the Americans with Disabilities Act, of federal appeals court judgeship.

Hopefully the Capitol Hill moratorium on criticizing missile defense will end soon, before additional billions are poured into this dangerous and unworkable project. And hopefully the current irresponsible attitude on Capitol Hill of uncritically throwing money at the Pentagon in the wake of the September 11th attack will be cast aside in favor of a vigorous public debate about the best way to prevent terrorism.

A missile defense system – even if it overcame the technical obstacles which have so far proved insurmountable, after billions spent – would have done nothing to stop the September 11 attack. Nor would it do anything to stop any other conceivable terrorist attack on the United States, none of which involve might missile delivery systems. Opportunism and cynical manipulation of tragedy are nothing new in Washington. But the proposals to exploit the September 11 tragedy for narrow corporate aims mark a new low. The United States is emerging from a national mourning period. Now is the time to proceed with caution and care, as the nation seeks to address legitimate security concerns (e.g., airport security) and tend to victims of the attack. It is no time to rush through proposals on matters essentially unrelated to the attack, especially damaging and foolhardy proposals that have been unable to win popular or Congressional support when the public has had a chance to consider them dispassionately, and on the merits.

"Although it has gone largely unreported, Afghanistan is in the grip of a three-year drought and on the verge of mass starvation. According to the UN-run World Food Programme, by the end of the year 5.5 million people will be entirely dependent on food aid to survive the winter -that's a quarter of the Afghan population... Let me be clear. The murder of thousands of innocent Americans has shocked and appalled us all. But any military action which disrupts the flow of aid to millions of equally innocent Afghans would be equally immoral..."

- Chris Buckley, Christian Aid Programme Officer for Afghanistan

— Proposes to reverse regulation protecting 60 million acres of national forest from logging and road building.

— Plans on serving genetically engineered foods at all official government functions.

— Appointed John Bolton, who opposes nonproliferation treaties and the UN, to Undersecretary of State for Arms Control and International Security.

— Nominated Linda Fisher, an executive with Monsanto, for the number two job at the Environmental Protection Agency.

ONE GUY, ONE RIFLE AND AN OIL PIPELINE
Bill McKibben

It's truly scary to imagine someone cooking up batches of anthrax and sending it through the mail. But the United States' deepest vulnerability to terrorism may have been exposed earlier this month not by a mad scientist or a suicide bomber but by a single drunken hunter with a .338-caliber rifle.

On Oct. 4, according to police, Daniel Carson Lewis of Livengood, Alaska, shot a single hole into the trans-Alaska oil pipeline. Because it was near the base of a long, gentle rise, strong pressure spewed 285,600 gallons of petroleum 75 feet into the air, saturating the tundra. The pipeline was shut for nearly three days as workers struggled to fix the leak.

Authorities quickly announced that Lewis was not a terrorist. "It was just somebody being stupid with their gun," a state police spokesman said. "Alcohol and a guy with a gun—nothing deeper than that."

99

If that was meant to be reassuring, it had the opposite effect. One guy with a rifle could shut down the biggest US oil pipeline, delaying 2.7 million barrels of crude? What if there had been half a dozen guys? What if they'd used something bigger than rifles?

And what if we had decided to drill in the Arctic National Wildlife Refuge? In the wake of the Sept. 11 attacks, and doubtless for reasons of profound patriotism, the Alaska congressional delegation and the oil lobbyists have been demanding opening up the refuge for oil production as a matter of "national security." They might as well paste a big "Kick Me" sign on Uncle Sam's back.

If industry estimates of oil reserves are correct, the 800-mile pipeline would for a few years carry as much oil as now moves through the Strait of Hormuz. It's hard enough to defend our oil supplies in the Mideast. It is impossible to imagine a fatter, or less defensible, terrorist target than the Alaska pipeline.

The classic study of US vulnerability, "Brittle Power," was carried out for the

---

— Nominated Michael McConnell, leading critic of the separation of church and state, to a federal judgeship.
— Nominated Terrence Boyle, ardent opponent of civil rights, to a federal judgeship.
— Canceled 2004 deadline for automakers to develop prototype high mileage cars.
— Nominated Harvey Pitts, lawyer for teen sex video distributor, to head SEC.
— Nominated John Walters, strong opponent of prison drug treatment programs, for Drug Czar.
Washington Post, May 16, 2001.

> "Judicial Watch, the public interest law firm that investigates and prosecutes government corruption and abuse, reacted with disbelief to *The Wall Street Journal* report of yesterday that George H.W. Bush, the father of President Bush, works for the bin Laden family business in Saudi Arabia through the Carlyle Group, an international consulting firm. The senior Bush had met with the bin Laden family at least twice. (Other top Republicans are also associated with the Carlyle group, such as former Secretary of State James A. Baker.) The terrorist leader Osama bin Laden had supposedly been "disowned" by his family, which runs a multi-billion dollar business in Saudi Arabia and is a major investor in the senior Bush's firm. Other reports have questioned, though, whether members of his Saudi family have truly cut off Osama bin Laden."
>
> - Author unknown

Pentagon by the Rocky Mountain Institute in 1982. Its authors, Amory and Hunter Lovins, wrote at the time that "all of the energy sources being promoted as the backbone of American energy supplies in the 21st century are precisely those least suited to survive the uncertainty and violence that seems likely to characterize the future." Amazingly, it's these same centralized technologies that the Bush administration pushed for in last spring's energy plan and continues to support.

The alternative, of course, is to take the money now used to subsidize fossil fuels and nuclear power and use it instead to jump-start the conversion to renewable energy sources, which by their nature are decentralized, flexible and unappealing to terrorists. Take, for example, wind power. It is already the fastest-growing power source on Earth, mostly because it's environmentally benign. But now we know it's a security asset as well. An enemy could knock

---

— Nominated J. Steven Giles, an oil and coal lobbyist, for Deputy Secretary of the Interior.
— Nominated Bennett Raley, who advocates repealing the Endangered Species Act, for Assistant Secretary for Water and Science.
— Is seeking the dismissal of class-action lawsuit filed in the US against Japan by Asian women forced to work as sex slaves during WWII.
— Earmarked $4 million in new federal grant money for HIV and drug abuse prevention programs to go only to religious groups and not secular equivalents.

out one windmill, but it wouldn't spew radioactivity and it wouldn't damage all the other windmills. No one is standing guard around the clock on their rooftop solar panel.

It's a happy coincidence that clean power is also secure power. The sooner we get to work on it, the sooner we'll be able to cross one item off our list of worries.

Reprinted with permission from the *Los Angeles Times*

"We have about 60% of the world's wealth but only 6.3% of its population. In this situation, we cannot fail to be the object of envy and resentment. Our real task in the coming period is to devise a pattern of relationships which will permit us to maintain this position of disparity. We will have to dispense with all sentimentality and day-dreaming. We should cease to talk about vague and... unreal objectives such as human rights, the raising of the living standard and democratization. The day is not far off when we are going to have to deal in straight power concepts.... The less we are then hampered by idealistic slogans, the better."

- George Kennan, Director of Policy Planning, US State Department, 1948

— Reduced by 40% the Low Income Home Assistance Program for low-income individuals who
— Nominated Ted Olson, who has repeatedly lied about his involvement with the Scaiffe, funded "Arkansas Project" to bring down Bill Clinton-for Solicitor General.
— Nominated Terrance Boyle, foe of civil rights - to a federal judgeship.
— Proposes to ease permit process, including environmental considerations, for refinery, nuclear and hydroelectric dam construction. *Washington Post*, May 18, 2001.

COLLATERAL DAMAGES

© Margarita Garcia 2001

"I came to America because of the great, great freedom which I heard existed in this country. I made a mistake in selecting America as a land of freedom, a mistake I cannot repair in the balance of my lifetime. "

- Albert Einstein, 1947

THIS IS NOT A TEST

The following transcript is from America at Risk, an "educational film" produced for the Space and Missile Defense Working Group, a division of the National Defense Industrial Association. The film was distributed to governors and top school officials in all 50 states. The missile-defense system, which ultimately will cost more than $60 billion, has yet to pass a realistic test.

SCENE 1 [Low, sweeping aerial views of strip malls and highways, fading into scenes of suburban streets: children getting out of school, riding bikes, playing soccer]

SCENE 2 [Bill, his wife and their daughter, Rachel, eating dinner]
RACHEL: Jimmy, this boy in my class, he spilled red paint all over his pants.

WIFE: Red paint?

RACHEL: Uh-huh. Mommy, can I please be excused?

WIFE: I guess so. [Rachel goes to play in the den.]

BILL: Have you seen all of the news about some of those third world countries? What are they called, "rogue nations" or something? [Close up of newspaper headline: MISSILE THREAT STILL REAL, EXPERT SAYS] There must be half a dozen countries all threatening to fire missiles at us, to keep us out of their business. You know, just like North Korea the other night, when we wanted to keep them from moving on South Korea. And just the other day China made that speech about us interfering in their new desire to take back Taiwan.

WIFE: Oh, honey, all that's just talk. You know, we hear it all the time.

BILL: Maybe so, but we've really gotten mixed up more and more in situations where countries threaten us with their ballistic missiles.

WIFE: Sweetheart, if they did fire something at us, we could handle it. We'd just shoot them down. They really can't get to us with those things, you know.

BILL: Yeah, but I've still got a bad feeling about all this talk of missiles being fired at us. There's been so much happening just in the past week. Tensions have gotten really high, and all that diplomatic stuff sure hasn't worked.

WIFE: Don't worry. There's been plenty of time and more than enough people to have already taken care of these things. Look, Bill, no one's going to do anything to us. We're the United States of America, for goodness sake! With all that money our country spends on defense, we've got it covered. Now come on, give me a hand. [Wife walks to sink]

SCENE 3 [Daughter stands in front of television holding a remote control. A news program ends, and an orange triangle appears behind the words STAND BY.] TV: This is not a test.

RACHEL: Mommy? TV: Repeat. This is not a test. [Cut to Bill and wife standing at sink]

BILL: Oh no!

WIFE: What's happening? [Bomb sirens sound]

BILL: I don't believe it. This is it. It's all over.

WIFE: Bill, where are we supposed to go?

BILL: There is nowhere to go!

WIFE: Then what do we do? Rachel, come here, baby! Now! Bill! What do we do? Please tell me! Bill!

RACHEL: Daddy? [Fade to white]

SCENE 4 [Montage of images with voice-over]

ANNOUNCER: It didn't have to be like this. [Footage of protesters] It could have been different. [Rachel's face in front of television, distraught parents, a Chinese rocket launching] How often do any of us remember that the threat is real? But the technology to defend ourselves DOES exist. [Military base, soldiers at computers] And the capability for a working missile defense HAS been demonstrated. [Computer image of missile shot from North Dakota intercepting missile shot from the east Atlantic] In fact, our government has proven that it can be done [Footage of a missile striking something and exploding] Now it's time to begin defending our nation from this threat. [Rockets launching] Don't let this opportunity slip through our fingers again. [Fade to black]

ENEMIES, BOTH FOREIGN AND DOMESTIC:
THE LIMITS OF REVENGE AND RHETORIC
Tim Wise

Well, it looks as if the good people of the rural US should be breathing a sigh of relief right about now. After all, with the President and most Americans itching to bomb any place where terrorists might be hiding, one can only imagine the kind of wrath that would have been brought down upon the heads of folks in Iowa, Nebraska, Wyoming or Mississippi had the guilty parties been white boys with crew-cuts, like Tim McVeigh. All this talk of "Kill the Arabs," "carpet bomb 'em back into the stone age," or "get the rag heads" would have to have been replaced with "Kill the Crackers," "bomb 'em back to the 'Dust Bowl,'" and "get the trailer trash." But the fact is, we all know that such a scenario would never have transpired, and not because white boys aren't capable of inflicting mass death. They certainly are. McVeigh proved that, if for some folks Hitler, Stalin, Andrew Jackson, Lyndon Johnson and Dick Nixon weren't sufficient to make the case. But rather, because the folks who are so quick to collectivize the responsibility and the payback when the perps are dark-skinned or "foreign," are just as quick not to do so when white boys are the ones committing mass murder or engaging in terrorist activities. In the wake of Oklahoma City, none of the people who are now calling for war against Afghanistan even suggested targeting white supremacist groups and militias for destruction, let alone bombing the cornfields of "middle America" in the hopes of taking out a few anti-government types.

© Daniel Massey 2001

Bottom line: Enemies who look different, speak a different language, or practice a different religion are lots easier to view as the "other." As if somehow cutoff from the common humanity of which we consider ourselves a part. And so we speak now of killing Arabs indiscriminately, of not differentiating between the guilty and the innocent (ironically, the precise mentality of whomever carried out last week's attacks), and winning a war, which we claim has been officially engaged. But we would have said none of these things had the perpetrators been internal extremists. We said none of these things about those who fit the descriptions of Tim McVeigh or Terry Nichols. We would never have heard columnists calling for profiling of white men, the way that reactionary crank and wanna-be pin-up girl of the right, Ann Coulter, called for the same against Arabs and Muslims this week. Actually, that wasn't all she said: she also opined that it should be the role of the United States to invade "their"countries, kill "their" leaders, and "convert them to Christianity." If these were the words of an Imam, calling for the forced conversion of Southern Baptists to Islam, we would call them the fanatical ramblings of a jihad-happy madman.

```
To: Jeremy Glick
From: Jee Kim
Subject: fear

it's started. You feel it in the air? Bombs, biological
terror, your next door neighbor as terrorist. The return
address on your anthrax infested mail is Mr. Evil/ Evil
Inc/ 5 Cave Road/ anywhere in the Middle East. Fear kid,
fear. And the collateral damages for us: civil
liberties, hate crimes, immigrant detention, etc.
one
```

THE RAIN OF SORROWS
Purvi Shah, Sakhi for South Asian Women

September 11th is a day that changed all of us. As a board member at Sakhi for South Asian Women, an anti-domestic violence organization based in New York City, I grieve for a long-time friend and fellow volunteer who worked on the 94th floor of 2 World Trade. Swarna Chalasani is still "missing": for me the word has taken on a haunting quality and signifies not the possibility of return but that I miss Swarna's presence in my life and will do so for the rest of my life.

Swarna gave so much love and attention to the Sakhi survivors she supported. She provided women who wanted to break free of violence a chance to do so, not only by offering emotional support but also by giving women facing violence financial assistance from her own pockets. By donating money to buy sewing machines or other resources, Swarna helped women strive for their dreams. The world will never know what it lost — what dreams never had a chance to become reality — as a result of the terrorist attacks on September 11th.

I want to thank the firefighters, police officers, and rescue workers who struggled to save so many individual lives — and in the process may have lost their own. Yet the people who are lost to the rubble of the World Trade Center, the Pentagon, or the crashed airplanes are the not the only victims of the September 11th terrorist attacks. After the second round of American bombing, four Afghan UN aid workers were killed when their building was destroyed. As the United States drops bombs over Afghanistan, the victims are also innocent Afghans who have been trying to escape a country torn by war and instability for more than two decades. How do we mourn the four Afghan demining workers lost in the ruins of their bombed building? How do we prevent further misdirected American attacks on humanitarian agencies such as the International Red Cross Center? How do we demonstrate the same value for individual lives that the rescue workers showed in New York City for people who live outside America?

© Lina Palotta 2001

We should start by safeguarding and respecting the people in our own communities inside the United States who are facing a racist backlash in the wake of the attacks. One Sakhi survivor braved verbal attacks from fellow residents of a mainstream shelter, women who asked, "How could your country do this? How can you support terrorists?" This survivor, a Muslim Pakistani, did not know how to confront the ignorance or racism or need to proclaim her innocence. Even more troubling is that no caseworker or shelter staff person jumped in to aid her. Many women we work with — Muslim women, women who wear traditional South Asian dress, and undocumented immigrants — have so much more to fear now (as do other American Muslims, Arab Americans, Sikhs, and South Asian Americans).

Since September 11th Sakhi and sister organization Women for Afghan Women have been busy planning peace rallies and memorials in New York City. By some accounts, more than 300 Indians, 150 Pakistanis, and 50 Bangladeshis were killed in the World Trade Center: these numbers do not even count the undocumented workers. At Sakhi and Women for Afghan Women, we have felt the need to create a community forum for families to grieve and come together in the hopes for creating peace. We sought to carve a space that condemned the violence of the terrorist attacks and advocated against further violence...

We Americans of South Asian origin also have to be afraid of the enemy from within. In the early wake of the attacks in America, Balbir Singh Sodhi, a Sikh gas station worker in Mesa, Arizona, and Waqar Hasan, a Pakistani grocery store owner in Dallas, Texas were shot by men who saw themselves as American patriots. Those working-class members of our community, those who work in public spaces such as grocery stores, gas stations, or taxis are especially vulnerable to random violence — racism justified as patriotism. In a nation founded on the idea of innocent until proven guilty, how is it possible that so-called patriots can justify taking another life or hurting another person in the name of America? These American vigilantes who are targeting their Muslim, Arab American, Sikh, and South Asian American neighbors and community residents are the ones guilty — guilty of committing hate crimes against innocent members of American society. This racism cannot be tolerated. No person deserves to be abused based on their physical appearance, ethnicity, national origin, or creed. Domestic terrorism must be stopped because all of us deserve equal protection under the law — these are the ideals we Americans cherish...

In the four weeks since the tragedy, more than 645 incidents of racial abuse against Muslims, South Asians, and Sikhs have been reported. Will justice be brought to those who have suffered racism unjustly? Those who are victims of hate crimes should report the violence in order to document the abuse and provide impetus for policy and educational actions. We must remember that after the bombing of Pearl Harbor in World War II, more than 120,000 Japanese Americans were dispossessed of their homes and belongings and rounded up into internment camps — simply because they looked like the enemy. While no such overt government action has been taken against those of us who look the current enemy, the Mobilization Against Terrorism Act includes provisions which would expand search and seizure and wire-tapping laws as well as say it is legitimate to indefinitely detain legal immigrants suspected of terrorism. After the September 11th attacks, the FBI received more than 100,000 tips of terrorist activity: you do the math. Most of these tips were probably given by people who "suspected" their innocent Muslim or South Asian neighbors. In a time when South Asians are being removed from certain flights due to racist fear, are we willing to let our civil liberties be curtailed — perhaps forever? As America fights in the name of democracy and freedom, we cannot let the structures of democracy and freedom crumble here at home.

Effects of the Anti-Terrorism Bill

1) Further erosion of the rights of non-citizens:

The proposed bill allows for the indefinite detention of non-citizen Americans. They would be detained despite a successful challenge to the government's case for deportation. In other cases, persons may be deported without ever knowing the basis for their charge, without knowing the substance of the charge, and therefore without any opportunity to confront and dispute the allegations against them.

2) Sweeping expansion of law enforcement authority to invade the privacy of Americans:

Considerably expands the authority of law enforcement to conduct wiretapping and electronic surveillance of Americans, eroding those basic protections that were designed to distinguish general law enforcement investigations from foreign intelligence operations. Judicial oversight would be minimal. The bills would also expand the government's authority to conduct "secret searches."

THE NEED FOR DISSENT
George Monbiot

Bin Laden's presumed guilt appears to rest on the supposition that he is the sort of man who would have done it. But his culpability is irrelevant: his usefulness to western governments lies in his power to terrify. When billions of pounds of military spending are at stake, rogue states and terrorist warlords become assets precisely because they are liabilities. By using Bin Laden as an excuse for demanding new military spending, weapons manufacturers in America and Britain have enhanced his iconic status among the disgruntled. His influence, in other words, has been nurtured by the very industry which claims to possess the means of stamping him out. This is not the only way in which the new terrorism crisis has been exacerbated by corporate power. The lax airport security which enabled the hijackers to smuggle weapons on to the planes was, for example, the result of corporate lobbying against the stricter controls the government had proposed. Now Tuesday's horror is being used by corporations to establish the preconditions for an even deadlier brand of terror.

This week, while the world's collective back is turned, Tony Blair intends to allow the mixed oxide plant at Sellafield to start operating. The decision would have been front-page news at any other time. Now it's likely to be all but invisible. The plant's operation, long demanded by the nuclear industry and resisted by almost everyone else, will lead to a massive proliferation of plutonium, and a high probability that some of it will find its way into the hands of terrorists. Like Ariel Sharon, in other words, Blair is using the reeling world's shock to pursue policies which would be unacceptable at any other time.

Civil liberties are suddenly negotiable. The US seems prepared to lift its ban on extra-judicial executions carried out abroad by its own agents. The CIA might be permitted to employ human rights abusers once more, which will doubtless mean training and funding a whole new generation of Bin Ladens. The British government is considering the introduction of identity cards. Radical dissenters in Britain have already been identified as terrorists by the Terrorism Act 2000. Now we're likely to be treated as such. The authoritarianism which has long been lurking in advanced capitalism has started to surface.

111

> **September Gallup poll results: 49 per cent of the American people said yes (49 percent no) to the idea that Arabs, including those who are American citizens, should carry special identification; 58 percent demand (41 percent don't) that Arabs, including those who are Americans, should undergo special, more intense security checks in general.**

The governments of Britain and America are using the disaster in New York to reinforce the very policies which have helped to cause the problem: building up the power of the defense industry, preparing to launch campaigns of the kind which inevitably kill civilians, licensing covert action. Corporations are securing new resources to invest in instability. Racists are attacking Arabs and Muslims and blaming liberal asylum policies for terrorism. As a result of the horror on Tuesday, the right in all its forms is flourishing, and we are shrinking. But we must not be cowed. Dissent is most necessary just when it is hardest to voice.

Reprinted with permission from *The Guardian*

THE DOMESTIC TERRORISM THREAT

Statement for the Record
Louis J. Freeh, Director
Federal Bureau of Investigation

On the Threat of Terrorism to the United States before the United States Senate Committees on Appropriations, Armed Services, and Select Committee on Intelligence.

The FBI views domestic terrorism as the unlawful use, or threatened use, of violence by a group or individual that is based and operating entirely within the United States or its territories without foreign direction and which is committed against persons or property with the intent of intimidating or coercing a government or its population in furtherance of political or social objectives. The current domestic terrorist threat primarily comes from right-wing extremist groups, left-wing and Puerto Rican extremist groups, and special interest extremists.

Left-wing and Puerto Rican extremist groups. The second category of domestic terrorists, left-wing groups, generally profess a revolutionary socialist doctrine and view themselves as protectors of the people against the "dehumanizing effects" of capitalism and imperialism. They aim to bring about change in the United States through revolution rather than through the established political process. From the 1960s to the 1980s, leftist-oriented extremist groups posed the most serious domestic terrorist threat to the United States. In the 1980s, however, the fortunes of the leftist movement changed dramatically as law enforcement dismantled the infrastructure of many of these groups and the fall of communism in Eastern Europe deprived the movement of its ideological foundation and patronage.

Canada is banning some Arab students from taking university chemistry courses. Authorities fear foreign students from countries including Iraq, Iran and Libya will use the knowledge for bomb-making and terrorism, reports *The Toronto Sun*.

Terrorist groups seeking to secure full Puerto Rican independence from the United States through violent means represent one of the remaining active vestiges of left-wing terrorism. While these groups believe that bombings alone will not result in change, they view these acts of terrorism as a means by which to draw attention to their desire for independence. During the 1970s and 1980s numerous leftist groups, including extremist Puerto Rican separatist groups such as the Armed Forces for Puerto Rican National Liberation (FALN – Fuerzas Armadas de Liberacion Nacional Puertorriquena), carried out bombings on the US mainland, primarily in and around New York City.

> **"Every anti-colonial struggle has eventually come home to the metropole. Think Puerto Ricans attacking the US Congress in 1948, for instance. Millions of people round the world think they know what really happened On Tuesday. Among them: those who now seek to charge Henry Kissinger for terrorism in Chile and elsewhere. Among them: those who have been bombed in Grenada, Libya, Yugoslavia, Panama, Afghanistan, Sudan, Iraq. There are many more who have not been bombed and may not sympathize with the ayatollahs of Iran who describe the US as the 'Great Satan' but who understand what the ayatollahs mean. The government of Cuba - never a friend of terrorists, in its message of sympathy with the American people was constrained to point out that Cuba has been at the receiving end of US sponsored terrorism for 40 years."**
>
> **- John Maxwell**

113

Acts of terrorism continue to be perpetrated, however, by violent separatists in Puerto Rico. Three acts of terrorism and one suspected act of terrorism have taken place in various Puerto Rican locales during the past three years. These acts, including the March 1998 bombing of a super-aqueduct project in Arecibo, the bombings of bank offices in Rio Piedras and Santa Isabel in June 1998, and the bombing of a highway in Hato Rey, remain under investigation. The extremist Puerto Rican separatist group Los Macheteros is suspected in each of these attacks.

Anarchists and extremist socialist groups – many of which, such as the Workers' World Party, Reclaim the Streets, and Carnival Against Capitalism – have an international presence and, at times, also represent a potential threat in the United States. For example, anarchists, operating individually and in groups, caused much of the damage during the 1999 World Trade Organization ministerial meeting in Seattle.

Special interest extremists. Special interest terrorism differs from traditional right-wing and left-wing terrorism in that extremist special interest groups seek to resolve specific issues, rather than effect more widespread political change. Special interest extremists continue to conduct acts of politically motivated violence to force segments of society, including, the general public, to change attitudes about issues considered important to their causes. These groups occupy the extreme fringes of animal rights, pro-life, environmental, anti-nuclear, and other political and social movements. Some special interest extremists – most notably within the animal rights and environmental movements – have turned increasingly toward vandalism and terrorist activity in attempts to further their causes.

WHEN TERRORISM IS NOT TERRORISM
Author unknown

State Department Counter-Terrorism Coordinator Michael Sheehan, speaking at a briefing on the 1999 Annual "patterns of Global Terrorism" Report, May, 1 2000:

SHEEHAN: Our definition of terrorism by the legislation is very explicit. But in general terms, in a war, if military forces are attacking each other, it's not terrorism. But if an armed terrorist organization attacks civilian targets, that's terrorism. So that is generally the breakdown. Or if you attack, it's also... a terrorist attack if you attack military people in barracks, such as Khobar bombings or the Marine barracks in 1982. Those are terrorist acts. Each case is taken on a case-by-case basis.

REPORTER: *So, for example, if the United States were to drop - what do you call them - cruise missiles on the people who where in barracks or in tents, as it may be, would that be terrorism? Could that be terrorism?*

SHEEHAN: No.

[laughter]

The laughter was not included in the transcript of the briefing released by the state department, but could be heard when this segment was played on C-Span radio.

© Sophia Eminence 2001

LIBERTY AT RISK
John Conyers Jr.

115

Like every US citizen, I was shocked and revolted beyond comprehension by the attack on our nation last week. We need to do everything within our power to find the responsible persons and parties, bring them to justice and end the blight of terrorism.

At the same time, we must all remember that just as this horrendous act can destroy us from without, it can also destroy us from within. Historically, it has been at times of inflamed passions and national anger that our civil liberties proved to be at greatest risk, and the unpopular group of the moment was subject to prejudice and deprivation of liberty. In 1798, Congress enacted the notorious Alien and Sedition Acts, making it a federal crime to criticize the government. In 1861, at the beginning of the Civil War, President Lincoln suspended habeas corpus, citing the need to repress "an insurrection against the laws of the United States." Ulysses S. Grant sought to expel Jews from southern states. World War II brought about the shameful internment of Japanese Americans, which even the Supreme Court failed to overturn. Unfortunately, our response in 1996 to the Oklahoma City bombing and to the first bombing of the World Trade Center does not portend well for today's discussions. Legislation that began in good faith as an effort to fine-tune our anti-terrorism laws turned into a legislative race to the bottom. It contained sweeping new limitations on habeas corpus for death-row and other inmates.

The legislation also severely narrowed the ability of persons fleeing for their lives from dangerous regimes to seek asylum. I sat through the hearings on this legislation and did not hear a single shred of evidence that proved that a single terrorist act could be prevented by limiting the ability of persons convicted in state court to obtain relief from unconstitutional convictions or by denying immigrants their due process rights.

> **"Despite severe restrictions on their resources and fund-raising abilities, an often-derided group of Californians is donating money to the East Coast relief efforts. From Death Row inmates at San Quentin State Prison to minimum-security inmates fighting on fire lines, thousands of convicts at 10 of the state's 33 prisons are giving money to the American Red Cross and to funds established for the families of fallen police and firefighters. Russ Heimerich, a spokesman for the Department of Corrections in Sacramento, said $22,700 had been pledged so far. More is expected as the word spreads to other prisons. Some inmates have tapped into their so-called trust funds, or prison bank accounts, where they deposit their wages from their prison jobs. The maximum pay is 37 cents per hour. Others, who have received permission from prison wardens to hold fund-raisers, are planning portrait, candy and art sales. Permission is needed because prison policy doesn't allow inmates to run businesses from their cells."**
>
> - Pamela J. Podger, *San Francisco Chronicle*

Meanwhile, many laudable provisions were dropped from the 1996 legislation at the behest of the gun lobby. We tried to include a provision allowing for broader roving wiretaps, as has been recommended by Attorney General John Ashcroft, but the conservatives could not stomach this expansion of government power. An exasperated Henry Hyde, who as chairman of the House Judiciary Committee had worked to keep some of the better provisions, was quoted as saying that many in his party "trust Hamas more than their own government." We also failed in our efforts to ban dangerous "cop-killer" bullets and to require that "taggants" (tracer elements) be attached to explosive materials and that unregulated explosive material (such as the fertilizer bomb used in Oklahoma City) be rendered inert. Instead, we were forced to settle for an ineffective study of these issues.

Certainly, we must update our counter-terrorism laws so that they reflect 21st century reality. But new expansion of government authority should be limited to properly defined terrorist activity or threats of terrorism. And with increased federal power, we must ensure accountability and oversight. We also need to drastically improve airport security by increasing the training and wages of airport personnel. That will mean increasing the role of the federal government and allocating more federal dollars to these needs.

I urge the attorney general to take a fresh look at expanding the federal law to cover hate crimes. Recent days have seen a spate of hate crimes against Muslims, Arab Americans and South Asian Americans. Two persons believed to be of "Middle Eastern" descent were killed in likely hate crimes over the weekend. If we are going to expand law enforcement's ability to pursue terrorists, we must not neglect the government's role in protecting Americans from vigilante violence. We are a nation of immigrants, and we are all in this together.

The keys to success in developing anti-terrorism legislation will be balance and prudence. History has taught us that we should not use the threat of violence as an excuse to suppress legitimate constitutional rights and liberties. As Benjamin Franklin stated, "They that can give up essential liberty to obtain a little temporary safety deserve neither liberty nor safety." We must ensure that these acts of terror do not accomplish in a "slow burn" what the fires of the World Trade Center and Pentagon could not – subversively destroying the foundation of our democracy.

The writer, a Democrat from Michigan, is ranking member of the House Judiciary Committee.

Reprinted with permission from *The Washington Post*

```
To: Jeremy Glick
From: Jee Kim
Subject: censorship/Big Brother

Have you heard about the Boondocks comics being cut from
a lot of NY area newspapers? The Daily News and Newsday
cut the ones that are critical or at least make you
think about everything going on. The Daily News cut it
for three days and Newsday ran older, less controversial
comic strips. Scared of serious political commentary or
of losing flag waving readers, depending on how you see
it, I guess.
```

A PERSONAL LETTER FROM THE ENEMY
Nadia Maiwandi

Let the bodies hit the floor in Afghanistan.
Let the bodies hit the floor in Iraq.
Let the bodies hit the floor in Pakistan.
Let the bodies hit the floor in Iran.
Let the bodies hit the floor in Yemen.
Let the bodies hit the floor in all of the UAE.
We should wipe this scum off the face of the earth!! I personally don't care about
their babies, mothers, brothers, dogs, cats, or whatever. They should all die a
horrible and torturous death and then writhe in the pits of hell for all eternity...

UNITED STATES OFFICIALS NEED TO DEPORT EVERY ARAB BACK TO THEIR DIRTY
SANDY ASS COUNTRIES SO THEY CAN BURN WITH THE REST OF THEIR PEOPLE.
DIE RAG HEADS!

The above sentiments have been overwhelming my email accounts since Sept.
11. I am a member of several Afghan or Muslim e-groups discussing the
continuing tragedies in our homeland or the true peaceful teaching of the
Qur'an. People outside these communities largely overlooked such groups. It
was of little concern until Sept. 11 when the forums became an easy target for
bloody calls of revenge. Suddenly, our membership numbers are doubling and
tripling, as cowardly hatemongers, nameless and faceless, crowd to wish for
our deaths. In the first couple of weeks, it was constant: Every five or ten
minutes another message came through, each more profane and bloodthirsty
than the other. And messages are still coming.

I am the child of Afghan immigrants, who came to America in 1966. Even
though I was born here and my first and only language is English, I am
constantly asked, "Where are you from?" and "How long have you been here?"
My 6-year-old nephew, Alec, now third-generation American, is quick with the
answer to the question he has been asked his whole life. I look at him, so
young and far removed from Afghanistan, and wonder if he even knows where it
is—where this mysterious "home" of his is which he will never visit.

Suddenly, I am not a cute little novelty anymore, but THE ENEMY. Me: The girl
with all the rock albums and the annoying Valley-girl vernacular?

But it is a change I know all too well, from the Iran hostages back in 1979 as a
grade-school child and all the hatred for Iranian people that followed, to the
bombings of Libya in 1985, the Persian Gulf War in 1991, till today. The shift is

sudden and deliberate. America needs to come together and unite against THE ENEMY, and I am that. "Where did all this racism suddenly come from?" a concerned American friend asked me. I smiled. "It's always been there," I told her. "It's just more acceptable to speak it now."

The Boondocks
© Aaron Mcgruder 2001

A CONTEXT OF HIS OWN
Michael Gerber and Jonathan Schwarz

"I really believe that the pagans, and the abortionists, and the feminists, and the gays and the lesbians...the A.C.L.U., People for the American Way, all of them who have tried to secularize America, I point the finger in their face and say, 'You helped this happen.'"
– Jerry Falwell, September 13th
"I sincerely regret that comments I made...were taken out of their context."
– Jerry Falwell, September 14th

Nine Possible Contexts
1. "...NOT."
2. "You know, I'm really high right now, so this may not make any sense, but..."
3. "Keeping in mind that today is Opposites Day, I emphasize that..."
4. "My son showed me this cool thing on Alta Vista, where you type something in English and then have the computer translate it into French and then into Spanish and then into German and then back to English – it's kinda like 'Telephone,' you know? – and something that made sense at the beginning will come out sounding like..."
5. "If an infinite number of monkeys typed on an infinite number of typewriters, one of them would write..."
6. "I want to take a break from the grim events of this week, and salute the brave people who've spent years making America a better and more tolerant

place. Who's done this, who's helped this happen? Well, I'll tell you:"

7. "An insane man off camera is pointing a gun at my head and forcing me to read this statement. Quote,..."

8. "Please join me in praying that, in the wake of this horrific tragedy, Christ's message of peace will prevail, our entire country can unite in compassion, not aggression, and that no misguided person will state..."

9. "I truly believe that if Osama bin Laden had been born in America, right now he'd be saying..."

MUSIC, WAR, AND TERRORISM
- The Editors of *Rock & Rap Confidential*

It began right after September 11, when the 1200-station broadcast behemoth Clear Channel Communications banned all music by Rage Against the Machine and issued a don't-play list of 150 songs, ranging from Nena's anti-nuke "99 Luft Balloons" to John Lennon's sublime "Imagine," with its lyric "I hope someday you'll join us/And the world will live as one."

Clear Channel protested that it wasn't really a ban but its true colors were revealed October 1 when the company fired Davey D from his post as Community Affairs Director at KMEL/San Francisco. For over a decade, Davey D, the world's foremost Hip Hop journalist, has put controversial issues and personalities on the air at KMEL. Will Steve Harvey at Clear Channel-owned KKBT be the next victim of the chain's sleazy quid pro quo with the government? (On September 13, just before the Clear Channel censors went into action, the FCC declared its intent to lift all ownership restrictions on broadcast chains).

On September 14, the Secret Service closed down Rage Against the Machine's website. Other musicians who voiced opinions not approved by the government came under pressure to retract them. Kevin Richardson of the Backstreet Boys apologized (kind of) because he asked during a Toronto interview: "What has our government done to provoke this action that we don't know about?" Moby apologized for saying that the people of New York had been "failed" by the FBI and CIA who "exist solely to protect us from this sort of atrocity."

Now we are officially at war. Music, which is fundamentally for peace, will come into increasing conflict with the government. That's all to the good, but if we don't find effective ways to support musicians, the sound of silence will become deafening.

THE FALLOUT
Jeff Chang

Sadeque was wearing red, white and blue. In the early hours of September 14, the postal worker was heading home to Brooklyn after his swing-shift job as a mail sorter. He was reading a foreign newspaper in a solitary corner of a packed subway car.

Maybe it was his thick beard. His dark brown skin. Maybe it was the foreign newspaper that would soon be covered in blood. Whatever it was, a tall, heavy-set white man stepped to Sadeque and began asking him something about the World Trade Center.

"Jeru Tha Damaja came out with an album in 1993-94 called 'The Sun Rises in the East.' The back of the album has a picture of the Twin Towers on fire. Plus Duo Live, same thing. The album was 'March Madness.' They have the Twin towers burning. That came out in 2000. We knew it would only be a matter of time before the center of the capitalist world caught some reciprocity for its ways and actions. Hip Hop being the voice for most poor blacks and Latinos, a catastrophe like 9/11 comes as no surprise to us seeing as how we saw first hand the corrupt and violent ways of our government, e.g., police brutality, ghetto life."

- Juan Pablo

121

Sadeque has only been in the US for four years, having won an immigration lottery that enabled him to bring his wife and daughters to New York. His command of English still isn't strong. He couldn't understand what the white man was saying. But now this man was in his face, saying something that seemed threatening. Trying to keep his composure, Sadeque groped for the right words, finally saying, "I am Bangladeshi."

Perhaps Sadeque thought that would cool out the threat. It didn't.

The next thing he knew he was knocked to the train's floor. Two or three men he couldn't tell were on top of him, repeatedly striking his head. Sadeque tried to use the newspaper to cover himself but blood continued to seep out of his nose and ears. "Help me! Help me!" he yelled. The other passengers on the crowded car simply stared.

Perhaps the men finally stopped pummeling him, perhaps he was finally Able to break away, he doesn't know for sure. But eventually Sadeque got up. His head was ringing. He stumbled to the end of the car, flung open the door and moved to the next one. He screamed for help and he searched for the conductor. There was blood all over his uniform.

As the train entered the next stop he looked back to see the men who had attacked him disembark. "When the guys who knocked me left the train, then everybody came to me," Sadeque recalls. "They said, We are sorry. We are sorry we [could not] help you." One woman gave him a tissue, another gave him a Tylenol, and Sadeque sat there fearful, confused and in pain as the train kept rolling. "The motorman told me, Do you need ambulance?? But I had no sense, what could I do? I am alone."

Sikhs, at prayer in Queens, wearing American flag pins
© Daniel Massey

Beyond the shadow of where the World Trade Center stood, there are new fears and targets of racial hatred. The dark fiery cloud of death was still blowing out of lower Manhattan when Arab, Muslim, and South Asian Americans were hit with racial profiling and racially-motivated violence. From Seattle to Tampa, Laramie to Mobile, stores and mosques were firebombed. Students were pelted with stones or shot at. Taxi drivers were taken out of their cabs and beaten. White-collar workers were suddenly demoted or fired without cause. Travelers were pulled out of trains and planes or stopped in their cars, and detained by authorities for questioning. Muslim women and girls in hijabs the traditional head-scarf Islamic females wear were chased by men who spat on them while screaming things like, "We'll kill you all!"

In the week following the attacks, the South Asian American Leaders of Tomorrow, an advocacy group, counted 645 separate media-reported bias incidents against people thought to be from the Middle East. By the end of

September, groups that monitor hate crimes against Arabs, Muslim, and Asians had logged nearly 1,000 separate incidents. Nationally, roughly half the tallied incidents were confirmed acts of violence, including beatings, stabbings, and shootings. At least five people were murdered, in places like Texas, Arizona and California, far from the rubble in New York City and Washington D.C.

As October began, the quantity and severity of the incidents seemed to wane, but there was a sense among Arabs, Muslim, and South Asian Americans that tension, suspicion, and fear were settling in for a long stay.

Pollsters found that a majority of Americans favor the racial profiling of people who look Middle Eastern. But many were surprised at just who seemed to supported racial profiling. According to a Gallup poll, African Americans favored racial profiling at higher rates than whites, 71% to 57%. "Maybe for the first time, Blacks and Latinos are seeing themselves eye to eye with whites," says Sin Yen Ling, an attorney with the Asian American Legal Defense and Education Fund. "It's United We Stand? except for Arabs, South Asians and Muslims."

123

Civil liberties advocates working to end racial profiling saw years of work rolled back after September 11. "The momentum has changed," says Ling, who has been documenting incidents of hate violence and racial profiling of South Asians. Van Jones, the executive director of the Ella Baker Center for Human Rights, adds, "Racial profiling has been legitimated in the minds of the public and in the practice of law enforcement in away that would have been completely unacceptable even a month ago."

And on the streets, civil rights advocates worried about the potential for inner-city racial flashpoints where Blacks and Latinos came into contact with Arab, Muslim and South Asians. As reports of fire bombings and shootings circulated across the nation, they asked themselves, what if the bill for all the daily humiliations like being unable to catch a cab or being profiled and harassed while shopping in the corner store had come due on September 11? Boycotts or protests now seemed meek. Cries of "Fuck them towel heads" could, absurdly, seem patriotic.

Before a friendly game of football in Fort Greene Park, Black and Latino teens from Bishop Loughlin Memorial High School talked about the Arab-run stores in their neighborhoods. "Ever since the bombing happened, people have gotten agitated to a higher level than what anybody ever dreamed," says Miqueo Rawell-Peterson, 17, of Far Rockaway. "The Arabs around my house just closed shop and moved on. I don't know where they've gone."

Still, the youths wondered if many storeowners sided with the terrorists against America. Edwin Ortiz, 17, of Far Rockaway, a Salvadoran whose cream-colored skin could make him look Egyptian, says the Arab clerk at his neighborhood bodega seemed happy about the attacks, smiling at him as he purchased a newspaper displaying the burning World Trade Center towers. While many store-owners had taken to hanging flags on their store windows, Louis Johnson, 18, of East New York believes "it could be a front."

Then the talk shifted to police. They said that the September 11 attacks had forever changed their perceptions of cops. "I guess we've become a little more at ease with the policemen," says Rawell-Peterson. "We realize what they've done. They were the first to the World Trade Center, besides the firemen. Now we look at them more as heroes, instead of I guess what you would say, enemies."

© Lina Palotta 2001

Louis says that cops used to harass him whenever he'd enter the subway station at Atlantic Avenue, located at the border between Fort Greene, a predominantly African American neighborhood and Cobble Hill, one of New York City's largest Arab communities. "Now, it seems like they don't really bother us. They stop everyone that has Middle Eastern features," he said. He adds that there is a new fear in the subway station." Everyone is still afraid to go on the train. I'm scared to go on the train because you don't know if the guy next to you has a bomb just waiting for it to go off."

Van Jones understands these sentiments, but, he says, communities of color must be critical of the mainstream American spin on terrorism because it can't be separated from racism. "All of a sudden Black and Latino youth are being considered Americans for the first time, in opposition to this new other? of Arab, Muslim, and South Asian people," he says. "I think that it's gonna require a whole new level of maturity and leadership for us not to jump on this bandwagon."

Mosques and social service agencies were faced with a wartime dilemma: having to coordinate aid and comfort for an embattled community while securing themselves and their property from hate violence attacks. Habiby-Brownesays, "We as a community who are part of the city, part of the society, Americans, taxpayers, voters haven't even been given the time to mourn, because we have been marginalized and isolated."

```
To: Jeremy Glick
From: Jee Kim
Subject: Re: censorship/Big Brother

Do you think we should be more careful with our emails,
esp. in a time like this? I have an amazing activist
friend who works on Palestinian issues and she got her
phones tapped literally 15 minutes after the first WTC
crash…
```

In the schools, especially, Arab, Muslim and South Asian American youths suddenly felt the heat of unwanted attention... Arab and Muslim students told painful stories of how they're being attacked and scapegoated for the "terrorists" actions. Nora Abdel-Nabi, a sophomore at Talents Unlimited High School in Manhattan, began noticing cars displaying signs that said, Death to all Arabs. Classmates that had never been patriotic before were suddenly saying things like,"Yo, son, we gotta nuke em all". She says, "The people who would usually say hello, they try to avoid me [now]. Some kid told me he had no respect for any Arabs. I didn't know what to say to him."

Salina Ali, a senior at Richmond Hill High School in Queens, watched news at home with her mother, and grew angry at media coverage of Palestinians allegedly celebrating the attacks. "I can understand why people are angry about it. We're also angry that the media would actually show that, because it triggered a lot of anger," she says. "The people that saw it, it made them angry and want to feel like they should go out and hurt someone or take revenge."

```
To: Jee Kim
From: Jeremy Glick
Subject: Fuck Big Brother

fear should make us smart, sharp, not scared p-noid, and
petrified. Yes, let's be strategic brother, but never
let detour become a permanent way of movement
```

She began worrying for her family's safety and begged her mother not to wear her hijab outside the house. And although Salina does not regularly wear ahead-scarf, her faith has also become a public issue. She says, "I felt really uncomfortable in my classes. My history teacher talks about Afghanistan and the war and Muslims. I just sit there and everybody knows that I'm Muslim. I actually got into an argument withal student. He started saying, You Muslims, it's because of you kids that we got attacked. One day it's okay, I feel like nobody's making any comments. But a few days later, it starts up again."

Until September 11, the hood around Atlantic Avenue with its restaurants and rug stores, markets and mosques was largely peaceful. Arabs from the old buildings on Atlantic and Blacks and Latinos from the nearby projects admixed easily, hanging out together, and going to the same clubs. Now shit was tense. Jawad"Lefty" Saleh, a 21-year-old rapper, had been born and raised there. In annual trips back to Jerusalem, he had seen what war was doing to his family in the Holy Land. Now his streets were undergoing their own kind of destabilization.

Now, old Black and Latino friends were stepping to him and his Arab friends calling them "Arab bastards" and "sand niggers." "Back in the days, I would have been like, Yo, I'm about to get him," said Lefty. "I'm not like that no more. You want to make your remarks? Make your remarks. A lot of pain going on." He was urging his homies not to respond to the new hostility, lest something start that couldn't be taken back. "As long as there's no physical contact, turn your face away," he told them." Cause when people are ignorant, people are ignorant. Can't change that now."

Us against the world. At one time, it was a slogan that united the Hip Hop generation against the culture war, the war on drugs, the war on gangs, and the war on youth. Now the generation has been torn apart by a war much bigger than Hip Hop.

But Van Jones believes that the Hip Hop generation has an important role to play. "Hip Hop has a special responsibility to educate the youth," he says." I think it's wrong for Blacks and Latinos to get taken down from the lynch tree and then applaud and be glad when somebody else gets put up there. I think we have a special obligation to oppose anybody being put up there. Every community of color has to be the darkies they love to hate for a little while. But we shouldn't be throwing rocks. Next time around it's gonna be us again. It's a merry-go-round of which one of us is gonna be at the bottom getting spat on. We just need to recognize that and not fall for it."

As he heals, Sadeque, who is Muslim, continues to pray five times a day. He can open his mouth now, although sometimes when he eats, sharp pains erupt in his right ear. When he kneels, he has a new prayer. He says, "I don't know what is happening in the future. I cannot imagine. We need peace now, no war. But I pray all of the time: May God bless America. May God bless all of us in the world."

```
To: Jeremy Glick
From: Jee Kim
Subject: Re: Fuck Big Brother

True indeed.

That's probably what Mohammed Ali was thinking when a
mob of reporters asked him when he was at ground zero
to pray for the thousands who lost their lives about how
he felt about the suspects sharing his religion, Islam.
Ali hit em with a quick left hook, snapping back: "How
do you feel about Hitler sharing yours?" Holla!
```

BUSH'S ORWELLIAN ADDRESS
HAPPY NEW YEAR: IT'S 1984
Jacob Levich

Seventeen years later than expected, 1984 has arrived.

In his address to Congress Thursday, George Bush effectively declared permanent war – war without temporal or geographic limits; war without clear goals; war against a vaguely defined and constantly shifting enemy. Today it's Al-Qaida; tomorrow it may be Afghanistan; next year, it could be Iraq or Cuba or Chechnya.

No one who was forced to read 1984 in high school could fail to hear a faint bell tinkling. In George Orwell's dreary classic, the totalitarian state of Oceania is perpetually at war with either Eurasia or Eastasia. Although the enemy changes periodically, the war is permanent; its true purpose is to control dissent and sustain dictatorship by nurturing popular fear and hatred.

The permanent war undergirds every aspect of Big Brother's authoritarian program, excusing censorship, propaganda, secret police, and privation. In other words, it's terribly convenient.

And conveniently terrible. Bush's alarming speech pointed to a shadowy enemy that lurks in more than 60 countries, including the US. He announced a policy of using maximum force against any individuals or nations he designates as our enemies, without color of international law, due process, or democratic debate.

He explicitly warned that much of the war will be conducted in secret. He rejected negotiation as a tool of diplomacy. He announced starkly that any country that doesn't knuckle under to US demands will be regarded as an enemy. He heralded the creation of a powerful new cabinet-level police agency called the "Office of Homeland Security." Orwell couldn't have named it better.

By turns folksy ("Ya know what?") and chillingly bellicose ("Either you are with us, or you are with the terrorists"), Bush stepped comfortably into the role of Big Brother, who needs to be loved as well as feared. Meanwhile, his administration acted swiftly to realize the governing principles of Oceania:

WAR IS PEACE. A reckless war that will likely bring about a deadly cycle of retaliation is being sold to us as the means to guarantee our safety. Meanwhile, we've been instructed to accept the permanent war as a fact of daily life. As the inevitable slaughter of innocents unfolds overseas, we are to "live our lives and hug our children."

FREEDOM IS SLAVERY. "Freedom itself is under attack," Bush said, and he's right. Americans are about to lose many of their most cherished liberties in a frenzy of paranoid legislation. The government proposes to tap our phones, read our email and seize our credit card records without court order. It seeks authority to detain and deport immigrants without cause or trial. It proposes to use foreign agents to spy on American citizens. To save freedom, the warmongers intend to destroy it.

IGNORANCE IS STRENGTH. America's "new war" against terrorism will be fought with unprecedented secrecy, including heavy press restrictions not seen for years, the Pentagon has advised. Meanwhile, the sorry history of American imperialism – collaboration with terrorists, bloody proxy wars against civilians, forcible replacement of democratic governments with corrupt dictatorships – is treated as strictly off-limits by mainstream media. Lest it weaken our resolve, we are not to be allowed to understand the reasons underlying the horrifying crimes of September 11.

The defining speech of Bush's presidency points toward an Orwellian future of endless war, expedient lies, and ubiquitous social control. But unlike 1984's doomed protagonist, we've got still got plenty of space to maneuver and plenty of ways to resist.

It's time to speak and to act. It falls on us now to take to the streets, bearing a clear message for the warmongers: We don't love Big Brother.

Originally published through the Common Dreams News Center (http://www.commondreams.org)

"The Pentagon has spent millions of dollars to prevent western media from seeing highly accurate civilian satellite pictures of the effects of bombing in Afghanistan. It was revealed yesterday the decision to shut down access to satellite images after reports of heavy civilian casualties from the overnight bombing."

- Duncan Campbell

WHERE DO WE GO FROM HERE?

Rockefeller Plaza, NYC
© Margarita Garcia 2001

"As we remember the victims of Black Tuesday, let us also strengthen our solidarity with the millions of invisible victims of other forms of terrorism and violence which are threatening the very possibility of our future on this planet. We can turn this tragic brutal historical moment into building cultures of peace."

- Vandana Shiva

TALK IS CHEAP, WAR IS EXPENSIVE
Vicki Robin, Coauthor, *Your Money or Your Life*

I've stopped my email activism for over a week. The world (and my inbox, the airwaves and the press) is full of analysis, advice, anger, imaginative solutions, poems, and more. Magically, every insight I've had has appeared within hours in someone else's words. Not only that, reputable sources forwarded Nostradamus predictions and a bogus letter of spiritual instruction attributed to the Dalai Lama (a Buddhist talking about God?), only to sheepishly retract them. Good time to think before sending. The initial shock is receding and blame is rising. It's the fault of: homosexuals, corporate globalization, Muslims, US foreign policy, people who don't hang flags, people who do. In a fit of unusual honesty, a military officer involved in planning said, "We're going to lie about things." People with scraps of data wander amongst each other, citing polls without sources and other media hearsay, allowing their own intelligence, bodies and souls to be whipped around in this maelstrom of quarter truths. Everyone is engaged in daily study of ideological "x-isms" and geographical "y-istans," trying to fathom their once safe world. Good time to listen deeply. But now I've got an idea. Hear me out.

"When we react out of fear and hatred, we do not yet have a deep understanding of the situation. Our action will only be a very quick and superficial way of responding to the situation and not much true benefit and healing will occur. Yet if we wait and follow the process of calming our anger, looking deeply into the situation, and listening with great will to understand the roots of suffering that are the cause of the violent actions, only then will we have sufficient insight to respond in such a way that healing and reconciliation can be realized for everyone involved."

-Thich Nhat Hanh

Some are using the metaphor of war (with very visible and, I deeply fear, predictable and sorrowful results). Some are using the metaphor of crime, with implications that we can bring terrorists - and terrorism - slowly to the mat through law not vengeance. I support this. Some are proposing the metaphor of contagion, that terrorism is a virus. This is very promising because we all have bodies and can relate and because the medical community is oriented to reason, verifiable results and healing. But here's another promising metaphor: school. The attacks were a tragic "F" in global safety. We are all in the School of the 21st Century and are going to learn together how to succeed in this brave, new, and dangerous world. In this School of the 21st Century we aren't competing for grades, diplomas or good jobs. It's bigger than that. If we "graduate" we get wisdom. If we fail, we fail collectively and our next "F" could be far more painful. We cannot kill enough people to end terrorism. We cannot jail enough to make the world safe. We've already learned the punishing lesson that we in the US are now part of the world community that lives with the daily terror of attack. Lessons aren't just painful consequences. They are also preparations for the future. So what do we need to learn in this School of the 21st Century?

First lesson: we don't know how to win, or even what winning is, in the 21st century. We have a diversity of opinions, often asserted as holy truth, but no certainty. We need a big dose of humility. Not blame of self or others. Just humility. Openness. Curiosity about what else, now that we've "tried everything," could lead us to stability. Second lesson: consult the experts. Thankfully, there are historians, social scientists, eyewitness informants, academicians, policy analysts, spiritual leaders and more who have gifted us with billions of useful words. Indeed, while some people turned to TV, others put books about Islam and Afghanistan and terrorism on the best-seller lists. Lesson three: turn to one another. Our natural inclination to gossip will bring us in contact with steady flows of hearsay. Hopefully, the self-correcting mechanisms of contrary facts will temper any false rumors. But the flow can't be stopped. Instinctively, people trust other people more than they trust the media or even the government. We also learn from others' personal stories, from their scholarly studies and from their soul-struggles. Conversation is education. Lesson four: turn to those who disagree with you. They are your teachers. The dissonance between my certainties and another's knowledge cracks me open, allowing my heart and my opinions to soften and fresh insight to flow in. In other words, I learn.

A friend once told me of her best, and most difficult, professor in college. He said, "I am not here to teach you. I am here to irritate you so you will learn." Where is the classroom for this essential School of the 21st Century? I suggest it is out in public with other citizens. Let every cafe become a classroom. Let public safety mean social trust as well as military might. I say, grab your grief and anger and take it to the 21st Century School of Co-education. Talk to people. Learn. Share your stories as though they were essential to the future of our world. They are.

133

**toppling from the heights
having a downturn in fortune
suffering a blow to the ego**

**having a revelation
suddenly realizing the truth
exposing what was hidden
having a burst of insight
seeing through illusions
getting the answer
seeing everything in a flash**

LEARNING FROM VULNERABILITY
Author unknown

A wise psychotherapist recently shared with me some of his thinking on crisis.
He said that in the field of developmental psychology a crisis is defined as an
event or period during which all that we know about ourselves and possibly the
world is violently ripped away. The self that we recognized yesterday in the
morning mirror is suddenly different. The world we understood last week as we
looked out the car window has been irrevocably transformed. New information
has entered our consciousness, be it the infidelity of a spouse or the toppling
of the World Trade Center, and we have absolutely no idea how to integrate it.
This can't be happening, we think. I knew this person better than that, we say
to friends. This could never happen in the United States!

In the space of confusion, loss, and abject pain, we often grasp hungrily at old beliefs, and try desperately to make our current reality look more like the familiar but now completely illusory landscape of the past. We can try to pretend that our spouse did not cheat on us, for example, or that the United States really is invincible and that being American makes us immune to certain kinds of horrible experiences. Fighting the new information, we think we are being strong, and that shielding our psyches from the new reality is the only available form of self-protection.

Another option is to allow the experience to work on us, to affect us irrevocably as well. As our minds reel and our souls work overtime trying to metabolize the experience and make sense of what has happened, we enter into a process of becoming. We are no longer who we were, but are rapidly becoming someone new, someone for whom this experience serves as an opportunity for growth. Couples can explore the roots of infidelity and grow even closer in their understanding of each other. In the wake of the World Trade Center tragedy, we can ask questions and try to understand why this has happened and how we feel about it. If we are honest, we may find ourselves face to face with the terrifying truth of our own vulnerability and mortality. We may find ourselves more in touch with the pain and suffering of the millions of people around the world and in our own country who have lost loved ones to wars of all kinds: military, economic, psychological. Stripped of our naivete, relegated finally to what we are, citizens of the world, we are moved to think more deeply about the impact of our actions on our brothers and sisters from Beirut to Belize, from Birmingham to Bombay. We can begin to understand even more deeply how connected we all, in fact, really are. Our blinders ripped away, we see more clearly who we want to be: people who want a just peace and not a militarily contrived one.

135

A DEEPER WOUND
Deepak Chopra

As fate would have it, I was leaving New York on a jet flight that took off 45 minutes before the unthinkable happened. By the time we landed in Detroit, chaos had broken out. When I grasped the fact that American security had broken down so tragically, I couldn't respond at first. My wife and son were also in the air on separate flights, one to Los Angeles, one to San Diego. My body went absolutely rigid with fear. All I could think about was their safety, and it took several hours before I found out that their flights had been diverted and both were safe.

Strangely, when the good news came, my body still felt that it had been hit by a truck. Of its own accord it seemed to feel a far greater trauma that reached out to the thousands who would not survive and the tens of thousands who would survive only to live through months and years of hell. And I asked myself, Why didn't I feel this way last week? Why didn't my body go stiff during the bombing of Iraq or Bosnia? Around the world my horror and worry are experienced every day. Mothers weep over horrendous loss, civilians are bombed mercilessly, refugees are ripped from any sense of home or homeland. Why did I not feel their anguish enough to call a halt to it.

> All I have is a voice
>
> To undo the folded lie,
>
> The romantic lie in the brain
>
> Of the sensual man-in-the-street
>
> And the lie of Authority
>
> Whose buildings grope the sky:
>
> There is no such thing as the State
>
> And no one exists alone;
>
> Hunger allows no choice
>
> To the citizen or the police;
>
> We must love one another or die.
>
> – W. H. Auden, "September 1, 1939"

As we hear the calls for tightened American security and a fierce military response to terrorism, it is obvious that none of us has any answers. However, we feel compelled to ask some questions. Everything has a cause, so we have to ask, What was the root cause of this evil? We must find out not superficially but at the deepest level. There is no doubt that such evil is alive all around the world and is even celebrated. Does this evil grow from the suffering and anguish felt by people we don't know and therefore ignore? Have they lived in this condition for a long time? One assumes that whoever did this attack feels implacable hatred for America. Why were we selected to be the focus of suffering around the world? All this hatred and anguish seems to have religion at its basis. Isn't something terribly wrong when jihads and wars develop in the name of God? Isn't God invoked with hatred in Ireland, Sri Lanka, India, Pakistan, Israel, Palestine, and even among the intolerant sects of America? Can any military response make the slightest difference in the underlying cause? Is there not a deep wound at the heart of humanity? If there is a deep wound, doesn't it affect everyone? When generations of suffering respond with bombs, suicidal attacks, and biological warfare, Who first developed these weapons? Who sells them?

Who gave birth to the satanic technologies now being turned against us? If all of us are wounded, will revenge work? Will punishment in any form toward anyone solve the wound or aggravate it? Will an eye for an eye, a tooth for a tooth, and limb for a limb, leave us all blind, toothless and crippled? Tribal warfare has been going on for two thousand years and has now been magnified globally. Can tribal warfare be brought to an end? Is patriotism and nationalism even relevant anymore, or is this another form of tribalism? What are you and I as persons going to do about what is happening? Can we afford to let the deeper wound fester any longer? Everyone is calling this an attack on America, but is it not a rift in our collective soul? Isn't this an attack on civilization from without that is also from within? When we have secured our safety once more and cared for the wounded, after the period of shock and mourning is over, it will be time for soul searching. I only hope that these questions are confronted with the deepest spiritual intent. None of us will feel safe again behind the shield of military might and stockpiled arsenals. There can be no safety until the root cause is faced. In this moment of shock I don't think anyone of us has the answers. It is imperative that we pray and offer solace and help to each other. But if you and I are having a single thought of violence or hatred against anyone in the world at this moment, we are contributing to the wounding of the world.

137

Love
Deepak Chopra, M.D.

Demonstration in Washington, D.C.
© Sophia Eminence 2001

WE ARE A RETAIL STORE...
NOT A PLACE TO MAKE A POLITICAL STATEMENT
The Inside Story of how Deepak Chopra's "A Deeper Wound" became a Full Page Ad in the *New York Times*
Paulette Cole, owner, ABC Home & Carpet

Deepak's email was forwarded to me. I read the letter and was moved very deeply. I've been a student of Deepak's for many years and I wrote him a letter, thanking him and explaining what a gift his words were in the face of this darkness. This was just a few days after, probably by the 15th. I realized I could be the conduit to allow this voice of consciousness to be heard. I told him I had two thoughts and one of them was to publish his letter as a full page ad in the *New York Times*. Deepak was enthusiastic and grateful for the opportunity to be heard in this forum. He felt that it was very important that the message be sponsored by my store, ABC Carpet & Home. I felt I would almost rather do it anonymously because I didn't want it to be self-serving in a publicity kind of way. Deepak felt that if the message was sponsored by a strong and separate entity in New York, it would lend credibility to the message and offer it a new channel besides his own network; ABC has nurtured its own cultural community. So I agreed, did the artwork, and sent it in to the *Times*. I got the ad in on a Thursday night for the deadline. It was all under a lot of pressure because we wanted to get it in that Sunday's *Times*.

Meanwhile, I share my business with two partners and we each hold entirely different visions. One of them is my father. One is my ex-husband. The day after the attack, my partners and I converted the production of our two restaurants to providing food to those working in the rescue efforts. We were brainstorming ways the store and its community could aid in the relief.

On Friday at 3 pm, I got a phone call from one of my partners who all of a sudden felt completely threatened and terrified and angry: "We are a retail store. This is not a place to make a political statement." He felt that I was endangering the well being of the business. In his eyes, I was putting our business on the line for this issue. Even the representative from the *New York Times* recommended that I withdraw the ad, thinking it might be more appropriate to offer condolences like the other retailers. My partner suggested that I remove ABC's name and sponsor it personally. Deepak and I were in dialogue throughout the afternoon, he offered a more benign solution to appease my dilemma with my partners to have the ad sponsored under "friends of compassion." Eventually my partner surrendered to my conviction and chose to trust. (Because that partner happened to be my father, it was a deep personal challenge and achievement).

I have a very close cousin who is a lawyer who spontaneously and magically appeared that afternoon, he became the catalyst for fear and insight to the current wave of anger in the environment. He read the letter and felt that it was so provocative he was convinced that the letter as shown might not only initiate fury but could also create physical risk for the store, the employees, myself or my family.

Fortunately, my intention was so heartfelt and I felt such an awakening of consciousness I stood my ground. However, I did feel a great level of fear and hesitation. At 10 pm on Friday night Deepak called again and asked how it was

Billboards in Times Square
© Margarita Garcia 2001

"The only antidote to fear is love. You're either in fear or in love. There's not really any place in between... The only thing that I would really pray is different is that we would not go back to our habits. How do we keep ourselves conscious? What do we need to begin to sacrifice? How do we live our lives differently? What would I really take to the street for? What would I change my lifestyle for?... I keep thinking of the women in Afghanistan and I keep thinking about: It's hard to keep a sense of urgency and deadline in front of you... it's easy to get complacent. I think Americans are so willfully naive about our effect on the rest of the world. I think maybe it's beginning to dawn on us that this isn't just going to go away."

139

- Nina Utne, Publisher, *Utne Reader*

going. I said we were going forward, sponsored by ABC. "The only thing," I added, "is my cousin is here and he keeps putting this thorn in my side insisting that the letter will provoke anger, so I need to open the question with you: 'Do we have the right to take a risk here if there is that possibility that one single person would get hurt?'" Deepak was reassuring as he had consistently been, reminding me of the deeper message.

My body had been shaking for hours; it was a huge personal challenge. I had friends who were evacuated from their Tribeca home staying with me but they weren't able to offer me any relief. I went to watch the last 10 minutes of the dramatically patriotic fundraising telethon on TV with them. Stevie Wonder (my hero) and Willie Nelson were singing "God Bless America" and there was no talk of peace or freedom. I was disappointed; I felt that people who usually stand up for their beliefs didn't use the opportunity to voice a plea for peace. I felt a tentativeness, a fear of appearing to be unpatriotic. Bush had just given his first national address and received a wave of unanimous support. I felt immobilized.

"So many of my business friends have been waking up in the morning asking themselves: Why is it I'm doing what I'm doing? What difference does it make?"

- Joyce Haboucha, Rockefeller and Company

140   The fear grew in me, but I felt compelled to trust and stand by my conviction and voice a call for healing in the face of conflict. I had this hauntingly relentless voice echoing in my head: "What does your life look like if you surrender to your fear? What does your life look like if you don't do this?" I realized I couldn't avoid this fear; I had to acknowledge its presence, honor it, and then choose. I was clear this was the moment of realizing my potential and my life purpose. So I chose to let the fear move through me and to allow the passion to prevail. I had to keep moving forward and accept the consequences.

At 4 am Saturday morning the phone rang. It was Deepak and he said, "I haven't slept all night. Can you pull the letter? Should we pull the letter?" I said I don't know if I can pull the letter but maybe I can edit it. It was to run in the Sunday paper. They were scheduled to print that section at 11:15 that morning and there was no one there until 10 am! So Deepak and I went through the letter and I pointed out what areas of the letter were most provocative and could be edited. He changed and redesigned his thoughts in his words. The ending was changed to: "is to make sure our every thought word and deed nurtures humanity." I kept calling the emergency number at the *Times* while Deepak called me from an airplane: "Did you pull the ad? Did you reach the Times?" Finally I got through to the *Times* and they were able to make the changes. It felt completely perfect when it was done.

A NATIONAL PEOPLE'S TRUTH COMMISSION
S. Brian Willson, 1999, Revised Sept. 2000

A commission to reveal the US Government's historical complicity in state terrorism, both at home and abroad, while covering up such activities with fallacious pretexts and "plausible deniability"

"You in the [United] States must say, at some point, 'We need something like a truth and reconciliation commission,' and say, 'What is the pain that is sitting in the pit of our tummy?'" –South African Bishop Desmond Tutu, Chair of the 1995-1998 Truth and Reconciliation Commission (TRC) in South Africa, 1998.

A Truth Commission would be an effort to sensitize the US American people to our authentic history. This includes reaching out to political representatives, people who operate the bureaucracies and institutions of government, the wealthy and those who profit from corporate forces, and most importantly, the people at the grassroots throughout the nation, in order to bring to light the violent assaults that have been committed by our government and corporations for more than two centuries harming people and ecosystems here at home as well as abroad. Massive national denial has enabled "Manifest Destiny," and its characteristics of arrogance and greed, to prevail ad nauseum. A number of essays of mine have attempted to disclose the uncensored version of our history, a history of a civilization built on three holocausts that have deleteriously effected people, and their lands and resources, all over the globe. When this history is occasionally referenced to it is merely considered part of an unfortunate past with little or no bearing on our contemporary behavior, values, and policies.

If we are to have a world based on sacredness, respect, and justice, as foundations for peace and genuine security (win-win), then clearly some radical changes in consciousness, values and policies must occur. Change happens when people or cultures acknowledge their history and awareness of how that history has hurt and damaged so many. And now it has become obvious, even to the imperialists who are honestly assessing the consequences of global capitalism on the Earth's ecosystem, that every living being is threatened by the continuation of this model of "savage" capitalism. A profound healing process is urgently in order, and it can begin with acknowledgment of how the US civilization was really founded and how it has really sustained itself, and just how harmful our civilization has been, both here and abroad, and that it severely threatens the future for all of us. Then we, as a nation, can begin to share in the grief, and the reconciliation, as we ask, over and over again, for

141

forgiveness. The time is ripe, despite our apparent arrogance gone mad, for creation of a national US Truth Commission to facilitate our healing process before more harm, perhaps irreversible harm, to the livability for our species on the Planet, is committed.

The Commission's mission would be to chronicle a genuine people's history of the United States. This would include documenting the more than 400 military interventions into more than 100 countries over a 200-year period and the more than 6,000 covert operations around the world destabilizing numerous popular movements and governments. It would include, of course, the holocaust history of our European ancestor's treatment of the Indigenous Americans and of the kidnapped Africans who survived their ordeal only to become chattel slaves, and the twentieth century record of global interventions, killing countless millions, including our current overt and covert meddlings. It would provide a more people's oriented (versus traditional academic) analysis of how and why this has happened, and how it affects us, spiritually, mentally, psychologically, emotionally, politically, and even genetically.

"I believe that we must ask the mainstream Islamic world for advice. We must go to them and ask them what they would have us do. And then we must listen to them, and deeply."

- John Robbins, author, *The Food Revolution*

A US Truth Commission would be part of a national healing process, assisting our nation and culture in becoming earnest in its desire to be part of a peaceful presence on the Planet, shared with 210 nations and 6 billion people. Creation of such a mechanism would result only because many organizations such as churches, community groups, schools, peace organizations, and military veterans, etc., and notable individuals, would take up the cause. Especially important is reaching out to the college community of students and teachers and asking the question: Do you think the US needs a Truth Commission to help our nation become part of a peaceful process rather than continually aggressing to preserve a greed model?

Greed, violence, and arrogance as cultural characteristics would have to be forfeited, and that requires that we understand how those traits have hurt us, and continue to hurt us. As we know from history one never knows what might become of small efforts that contain the seeds of truth and love amidst the sea of insanity and violence. Life is unpredictable, no matter how much analysis we attempt from "objective" circumstances. Our integrity, consciences, and survival are at stake as human beings on Planet Earth. Creation of a US Truth Commission and the idea of it being sponsored and/or initiated by people such as US military veterans, historians, and clergy, among other constituencies, is presented here in the hopes of generating a movement for truth-telling in a nation steeped in denial.

Excerpted from: www.MennoLink.org/peace/sept11_top.html

CLOSE THE BOOK, GET UP, GO
Amy Cirincione, Wesleyan student organizer

On the night of September 11th, I cut the CNN umbilical cord and went to a meeting of college activists to figure out what to do. I sat in that meeting for an hour and half, listening to people plan a coordinated action to protest military retaliation, one that would unite people all over the country. One girl raised her hand and said, "I think we need to get in contact with other small liberal colleges. That's where we're going to find people who think like us."

143

I went outside to get some air. I couldn't breathe deep enough to clear my head, so I didn't go back in.

A coordinated action with a thousand like-minded college kids is about as revolutionary as a PTA bake sale. If you are a college student fiending for a revolution, you won't find it in your student union. You'll have to leave your campus and go someplace that you are scared to go. A place where no one cares about your diploma. Go to a union meeting or a shelter. Go to a city high school or a community center. Don't go as a tutor or a volunteer. Don't hide behind a community service program. Find friends who don't look like you, and sure as hell don't think like you. Go to learn that you don't know shit.

The liberal arts college label marks you as "one chosen to educate the less fortunate." It assigns to you the role of provider and savior and others the role of dark victim to maintain order and division.And that system assumes that we will never rise up against a common enemy because we will never realize that we have anything in common.

Prove them wrong. Become part of a coordinated action between high school students, single mothers, the homeless, and victims of police brutality. Join the other anti-war movements, the struggle against The War on Drugs, the War on

Social Services, the War on Minimum Wage, and the War on Public Schools. If we want to fight the war, then we have to fight all of them.

Close the book, man. Get up. GO.

We have a lot of work to do.

15,000 Peace March from Union Square to Times Square, October 18
© Margarita Garcia 2001

IT'S SIMPLE. IT'S NOT SO SIMPLE
Cynthia Peters

Now is the time to be talking to people.

Communicating, sharing information, listening – they are the core of social change, of changing minds, of exchanging rationalizations and cynicism for vision and empowerment.

It's simple, really. A terrible crime is being committed in our name. Millions of dollars worth of bombs are raining down on an already decimated country. Beyond the military terror and destruction, the terror of starvation almost surely awaits millions of Afghans unless the bombing stops and a full-scale aid program gets food in place for the winter. This is a calculated crime against humanity that differs from September 11th only in scale, i.e., it is many times larger.

That the US is taking part in the killing of innocent people is not new. What's new is that people are paying attention. Before September 11th, I tried talking to people about the 500,000 Iraqi children dead thanks to the US economic embargo. And people's eyes glazed over. But during these last few weeks, as I've staffed an information table on the main street that runs through my town, I've noticed something else during my conversations with people about the war in Afghanistan: the certainty of mass starvation unless our current trajectory in that country is reversed, the principles of international law, the idea that escalating violence is exactly that and not a form of justice, and the importance of the rule of law over the muscle of vigilantism.

What I've noticed is that the glaze is gone.

People's eyes are opened to the world in a way they weren't before. People are bringing questioning minds to the problem of terrorism and the US role in the Middle East and elsewhere. People are filled with grief, awed by the courage of the rescuers, stunned by what it means to turn a commercial jetliner full of innocent people into a living, breathing bomb. People are curious – and I mean that – about exactly how the US has abused its power around the globe, and they are reflecting on the consequences of that abuse.

145

Many conversations are not that hard. Sometimes, just listening to the words pouring out of someone's mouth helps him or her listen to those words, too, for the first time. Sometimes re-phrasing what you hear, without necessarily making a speech complete with historical facts and figures, is enough to put a crack in the confident parroting of the war defense. Sometimes, just being out on the street with "Justice Not War" flyers is enough to reach the cynic who already understands the misuse of US power but believes there's no point in contesting it.

But not every conversation is so easy. I don't feel good about having some guy towering over me, jabbing the air with his finger, spitting out his passionate belief that, yes, we should kill as many Afghans as possible. It's not just that it's personally threatening or that it's ethically in line with Osama bin Laden. It's also that it's painful to come face to face with this particular kind of human being.

Heartless retaliation is not limited to this war-mongering type. Consider the educated guy in the corporate suit who speaks in soft tones and has a pained expression on his face as he shrugs off the possibility of millions of starving Afghans with, "Well, we have to get Osama bin Laden somehow, don't we?"

Rather than scream my disbelief back at him, I try calmly repeating his own logic back to him. "So you think it's okay to put millions of Afghans at risk of starvation in order to possibly catch one man?" Then I try to let the pause be. I try not to fill up the silence with more words. I try to let him hear what he's saying. But this is hard to do. I feel a sort of a panic rising up. He is a thinking person, yet he articulated his accord with an obscene and murderous set of policies. I hold down the panic. He backs off a little from his argument. The interaction ends.

Unlike protesters in many countries, I don't risk getting killed or imprisoned when I put up my card table on Centre Street. I'm not worried about getting hurt, and I have a thick enough skin to deal with the hecklers. But dissent has its challenges, such as having reasonable conversations with privileged people who have access to power and knowledge, but who nonetheless are aligning themselves with points of view that will almost surely result in mass murder.

"A time comes when silence is betrayal. Even when pressed by the demands of inner truth, men do not easily assume the task of opposing their government's policy, especially in time of war. Nor does the human spirit move without great difficulty against all the apathy of conformist thought within one's own bosom and in the surrounding world. Moreover, when the issues at hand seem as perplexing as they often do in the case of dreadful conflict, we are always on the verge of being mesmerized by uncertainty. But we must move on."

- Dr. Martin Luther King Jr., Riverside Church, New York City, April 4th, 1967

This is where it becomes not-so-simple. I don't like talking to people like that man in the suit. They make me sick.

But talking is what we absolutely need to be doing right now. It is the only way to prevent mass murder. In a one-superpower world, the citizens of the superpower are the only force that can control the superpower. It's up to us.

Talking has the added benefit of being the only antidote to the sick feeling. For all the corporate suits, there are many more thoughtful people who pause, look me in the eye, nod their agreement that violence begets violence, say things like, "Thank you for being out here." "I realize I've never quite thought about it that way." "Do you have more information?" "Can I come to your meeting?" "Will you speak at my church?" "Where can I learn more?"

Many people I've met in the last few weeks don't need to hear my analysis. They already know. And they have a lot to teach if we listen. The Vietnam vet challenges me on how we should pressure our government when it is corporations that seem to have so much control. The firefighter tells me that all he hears at work is that the killing should stop. The Haitian man wonders how international legal channels could be made more independent and less influenced by the United States. The three women carrying bibles talk for a long time, first with me and then amongst themselves. The teenager starts off protesting that her parents would disagree with me, but winds up voicing her own views...

147

It's not hard to grasp the potentially genocidal consequences of current US policy. But it is a bit harder to integrate that understanding into your daily life, and let it affect your actions. How will this knowledge change you? What will it make you question about how you spend your time, what you do with your money, whether you are doing everything in your power to reduce the horror. Maybe before, when you sheltered yourself from this knowledge, you never wondered if it was okay to spend time watching the Yankees game. Now you are wondering.

And you are looking around at the peace activists and realizing that working in coalition with people to stop a major atrocity can mean aligning yourself with people you don't agree with – or even who you find personally threatening. Some of the people fighting this war might be the same ones that, in another forum, would be your boss, deny you a living wage, ensure more privileges for the already privileged. Some of your fellow peace activists would be horrified by your sexuality, find you perverse, or wish you out of existence. They may have never learned to listen to women or take people of color seriously. You survey the growing legions of peace activists and wonder if they're the same people who are gentrifying your neighborhood, planting tulips in the park but letting affordable housing go down the drain, never showing up to protest police violence or the gutting of welfare. Working with these people can be alienating, disheartening, downright soul-killing.

Should you do it anyway?

To answer that question, keep in mind that there are ways to ease this necessary work of talking and listening, putting ourselves face-to-face with brutal, merciless, or just plain petty thinking, and risking fragile coalitions.

1. Pick the community you can work best in. There is a growing peace movement, but if that is not your political "home," then work elsewhere – in your neighborhood, your union, your place of worship, your community organization. Don't stop doing the political work you were doing before, but do look for new connections. Now is the time.

2. We should appropriately acknowledge the frustration and alarm that will be part and parcel of organizing work, but we should also be careful not to overstate it. No matter how alarmed we might be by people's denial, people's rejection of a moral stance, people's downright selfishness, nothing compares to the alarm of those at the receiving end of US bombs and US orchestrated starvation. Keep your frustration in perspective.

3. Join others for solidarity, support, shared inspiration, venting opportunities, perspective, and retreat from the challenges. Know that organizing is painstaking work and you need to create conditions that will allow you to do it for a long time.

4. Know when to walk away. You don't have to talk to everyone. Don't waste time and energy engaging with the person who is going ballistic, but use your energy instead for the many sensible people that have their hearts in the right place but who lack information or support for entertaining alternative points of view.

5. Don't judge every interaction. It may feel like you failed to reach someone, but people's growing consciousness doesn't follow a linear path. They may ignore you but later privately read the literature you hand out, and this may affect how they read the newspaper the next day. Each step is exactly that, and with others adding their efforts, each step matters more.

6. Finally, pick the work you can do most effectively. If a two-hour tabling stint on your main street leaves you feeling drained, despairing or frightened, then do something else. Write an emergency grant to help pay for all the leaflets and posters. Volunteer to manage the database for your organization. Set up the web site, collate the articles, moderate the list serve, host the house parties, bring food to the meetings, design the banners, or take part in any of the numerous background activities that are essential to movement building.

Sound simple? It is and it isn't. Each of us, individually, has a responsibility to figure out how we can negotiate the organizing challenges and moral imperatives of the current crisis. Together, our job is to knit our individual abilities into a mass movement that pressures our government to back off from its bloodletting. The not-so-simple problem with this mandate is that it won't be easy. The simple fact, however, is that we must do it anyway.

Michael Franti of Spearhead
© David Hanks/Global Exchange 2001

TO COLORLINES READERS
Bob Wing, editor, *Colorlines*

I am by no means an authority on military or foreign affairs and these are just my personal opinions, but for what they're worth, here are some notes. I believe the Sept. 11 attacks are ushering in a major rightwing offensive, both global and national. It is likely to be sustained for some time and become a historical watershed. The rightwing of the ruling class and its ultra-right allies could not have asked for a better opportunity to aggressively move to reshape the world in their image.

149

Although progressives have been thrown deeply on the defensive, there are also openings to be part of the public discussion, if we are bold as well as very careful. We must be bold in building extremely broad coalitions, bold in attempting to enter the biggest media and political platforms. If we craft our messages correctly, we have many allies, and we should aggressively pursue working with them. We should not self-isolate. Peace, international solidarity, religious, anti-globalization, student, and civil rights groups should be approached. We should also use this opportunity to get labor, women's, anti-racist, and community organizations that tend to eschew international issues to get involved. This new situation will affect everyone to the core. We should actively build broad coalitions, not be content to hang on the left, hold "small but militant demonstrations" and expect others to come to us. We should try to get to the forefront of the fight for peace and basic democratic rights, spearhead large scale education campaigns, and get government bodies on record for peace and against unwarranted racist attacks on Arabs and South Asians. But we must be extremely careful about our public messages (and our

"On a movement level, I think it's really time for building. I don't think we need to be as out front in the media as we have been around anti-corporate globalization. I think it's time for us to build internally and build solidarity. Build a truly international movement. And we're gonna be talking about global justice and global policy in a way we never have. In order to meaningfully intersect with this new permanent war, we'd better be ready to play at a level we never even dreamed of before."

- John Sellers, Ruckus Society

internal rhetoric), lest we isolate ourselves and even make ourselves vulnerable to physical attack. We need to demonstratively express deep grieving over the death, destruction, and loss of security felt by most Americans. Most of us genuinely feel this, but sometimes we do not express it properly.

150

Almost everyone in the country knows someone that was somehow directly affected by the attacks, and all of us know in our hearts that life will never be as safe as it once seemed. Symbolism and emotions tend to run higher than rationality at times like this, and if we do not understand this, it will be difficult to get a hearing on other issues. We need to avoid leftwing rhetoric and revolutionary posturing, be concrete and address actual issues on the public agenda and not make premature anticipations or apocalyptic predictions. Internally we need to try to see as far ahead as possible and try to go deep analytically in order to be as prepared as possible, but externally we need to speak to facts on the ground, avoid concepts or images that are adamantly rejected by even peace loving people, and avoid prematurely polarizing with potential allies. All this while still drawing firm lines against the right.

I believe, at this time, we have two main entryways into the broad public discussion. By far the most important is by addressing the issue of why this attack happened and how to respond. Even the mainstream media is increasingly addressing this question, in its own ways. I believe our main message should be that US life will become increasingly insecure and dangerous unless this country improves its international behavior. In the era of globalization, peace at home is linked to peace abroad. And increased insecurity would likely result in lost civil liberties. We need to oppose a precipitous response by the government to the September 11 attacks and urge restraint. We can no longer allow our government to make war on others without expecting retaliation, whether one thinks that retaliation is fair or not. Peace and freedom are increasingly globalized, or not. We need to oppose US isolationism and aggression. Our loss of life should lead not to an eye for an eye, a tooth for a tooth, but to join others who have experienced war in the aspiration for peace. In taking on these issues, we should studiously avoid leftwing shorthands like "chickens come home to roost" (which will be read as a justification for the mass deaths of innocent people) and "no justice, no peace" (which will be read as a justification for further attacks). Peace, No Violence, etc. are much more directly to the point. What we are talking about is a new kind of peace movement.

The second main entry way is through opposing attacks on Arabs and South Asians in the US Such attacks are already underway, and are even being widely addressed by political leaders, civil rights groups, and the mainstream media. Again, building broad coalitions and using popular language is key. We should appeal for peace, fairness, and oppose violent racial stereotyping. I actually think that the more farsighted sections of the ruling class will want to stem these attacks so that their broader offensive does not lose the moral high ground. Minimally, they must make a nod in this direction. We should take full advantage of this opening.

151

While responding immediately to these huge events, we also need to embark on deep thinking about the implications for the future. What are the implications of this new situation for our attitude and strategies towards war and peace, how do we distinguish between the government's overbroad definition of terrorism and actual terrorism? How will the ruling class and public react and what platform can we stand on? What about the copy cat lunatic fringe and ultra-right fanatics who until now has confined themselves to comparatively small-scale shootings (except for Oklahoma City)? How do we break the fragmentation, disorganization and isolation of the left under these harsh conditions?

Finally, we should all be prepared for events to move fast. In particular, when the US mounts its counterattacks (which I believe is likely to eventually include the murder of Saddam Hussein), a wave of jingoism (and racism) is likely to sweep the country. We need to work hard ahead of this wave, prepare to weather it without getting too terribly isolated, and smartly fight our way through it. We're in for hard times, and our allies abroad even more so. We will all be struggling to find our bearings. We will make mistakes. Let's be tolerant of each other, keep our eyes on the real enemies, and seek clarity and unity. Let's think big and get organized. Maybe we can build something for the long run. I hope this is helpful to you in some way. Feel free to share it with others if you deem it useful.

In peace and solidarity,
Bob Wing

WHERE DO WE GO FROM HERE?

Joshua Karliner
Excerpted from www.CorpWatch.org, October 11, 2001

The events of September 11th and their aftermath have put activists addressing the ills of globalization in a terribly difficult position. What was an increasingly dynamic and effective international movement to place human, labor and environmental rights above unfettered trade and corporate profit, finds itself struggling to make its way out from under the metaphorical rubble of the World Trade Center.

The kamikaze terrorists chose their two targets in Washington DC and New York for their symbolic impact. Therein lies part of the problem for those of us challenging the injustices of the global economic system. The World Trade Center, the scene of this devastating crime against humanity, was also emblematic of a global economic system that has evoked massive protests by trade unionists, environmentalists, farmers, consumers, students and just plain folks from Seattle to Chiang Mai, Cochabamba, Prague, Quebec, and Genoa.

So it is critical for our movement – one of the most significant international social movements to emerge in recent decades – to strongly differentiate itself from the homicidal religious fundamentalists who struck at and paralyzed the nerve center of global capitalism. At the same time we must somehow continue to build (and to rebuild and reconfigure) our initiatives for local and global justice.

I think the movement for a different kind of globalization faces at least three fundamental challenges in the post-9-11 world:

1. To assert the relevance of our issues in a sophisticated and nuanced way that does not alienate
the hard-won public support gained since Seattle, and express solidarity with the growing list of victims, be they commodity traders, firemen, Sikh gas station attendants, or Afghan civilians.

2. To defend ourselves and others from a new trend which might be called "terrorist-baiting."

3. To regain the initiative in this global debate by building a platform for peace, justice and grassroots globalization.

If we can adequately respond to these challenges, the increasingly broad-based, decentralized, international coalitions that have emerged in the last several years may, in fact, become an important force in the creation of a more just, peaceful and secure world. If we cannot, we risk becoming marginalized – a mere footnote to an ongoing narrative of injustice and war.

"We need to make sure that the tide of patriotism sweeping this country is defined to include social justice and environmental sustainability. The tide is sweeping. We've got a patriotic tide going in here so we've got to make sure that we own it."

- Alisa Gravitz, President, Co-op America

Challenge 1: Finding a New Relevance

153

We cannot afford to be paralyzed. For the Bush administration is placing globalization at center stage. Calling for a campaign to "fight terror with trade," US Trade Representative Robert Zoellick has spearheaded an all out effort to take advantage of the post September 11th political moment and push fast track authority through Congress. The US is also lobbying hard to open a new round of trade negotiations at the upcoming WTO ministerial in Qatar.

Globalization, we have always said, is actually creating greater poverty and dislocation, exacerbating environmental destruction, undermining democracy as it caters to global corporate interests. The globalization of corporate media also flaunts our affluence while broadcasting a narrow, distorted picture of Western culture to nearly every corner on earth. The economic model Zoellick touts may be sowing the seeds of terrorism in the long-run.

It is our movement's responsibility, while maintaining solidarity with the victims of 9-11, to examine and articulate the specific globalization-related components of this crisis as part of a bigger picture. Indeed, in this respect, globalization is now more relevant than ever.

Challenge 2: Terrorist-Baiting

The anti-corporate globalization movement – the movement for a more democratic "grassroots globalization" – is being either explicitly or implicitly, but certainly falsely, linked to the terrorist attacks.

Peace rally in The Hague, Netherlands
© Jan Blankenstein/Stichting Amsterdam Photo Art 2001

Irresponsible slings and arrows began to fly on September 11th when US Congressman Don Young of Alaska suggested that instead of Islamist extremists who were responsible for the acts of terror, there was a "strong possibility" that it was the work of anti-globalization protestors. United States Trade Representative Robert Zoellick dangerously began to paint critics of free-trade as un-patriotic: "We will not be intimidated by those who have taken to the streets to blame trade – and America – for the world's ills." Corporate-globalization booster Reginald Dale concludes in an op-ed in the International Herald Tribune: "While they are not deliberately setting out to slaughter thousands of innocent people, the protestors who want to prevent the holding of meetings like those of the IMF or the WTO are seeking to advance their political agenda through intimidation, which is a classic goal of terrorism."

Not unlike red-baiting of the Cold War era, this terrorist-baiting of what is an overwhelmingly peaceful, democratic movement, is a dangerous trend that could have serious implications not only for the future of dissent and democratic debate, but also for the safety of the dissenters themselves.

To combat terrorist-baiting and keep it from becoming a more pervasive and dangerous phenomenon, the movement against corporate-driven globalization should take several steps. It is vital, for instance, to counter irresponsible statements such as those quoted above. It is also key to demonstrate solidarity with others who are already victims of the racist backlash in the wake of the attacks, especially South Asians, Arabs and black Muslims.

The movement must also now, more than ever, be unequivocal in its commitment to non-violence, and in condemning and preventing any violence from its own ranks – be it window smashing, dumpster burning, rock throwing or attacks on police.

I also believe that it is critical to clearly underscore the ideological differences between ourselves and the religious fundamentalists who carried out the attack on the World Trade Center... The divergences between these constituencies and our movement are clear. We are for a different kind of globalization; the fundamentalists are against globalization altogether. We are internationalists; they are most often nationalists. We are for openness, transparency, democracy, diversity and tolerance; they are almost always characterized by secrecy, xenophobia, homogeneity, and intolerance of the "other."

"I am convinced that if we are to get on the right side of the world revolution, we as a nation must undergo a radical revolution of values. We must rapidly begin the shift from a thing-oriented society to a person-oriented society. When machines and computers, profit motives and property rights, are considered more important than people, the giant triplets of racism, extreme materialism, and militarism are incapable of being conquered."

-Dr. Martin Luther King Jr. Riverside Church, New York City, April 4th 1967

155

Challenge 3: Regaining the Initiative

Unsettling as these times may be, we can't just react to the shifting political terrain. Of course, we must redouble our efforts to halt fast track, stop proposals for drilling in the Arctic National Wildlife Refuge, and prevent a new round of World Trade Organization negotiations. But we also must come up with an agenda of our own that addresses the suddenly changed times in which we are living and that allows our movement to regain the initiative which we saw disintegrate with the collapse of New York's Twin Towers.

The following are key areas from which we can begin to rebuild and redefine that agenda.

Peace and Non-Violence: Our movement for a different kind of globalization needs to call unequivocally for peace with justice...

It is critical that the anti-corporate globalization movement join forces with a broad array of constituencies fighting to protect democratic rights... This means not only standing up for civil liberties, but also against racism.

Global human rights. As global geopolitics undergo tectonic shifts, we must not ignore those who fall through the massive cracks that come with the new territory. As Russia realigns itself with the United States, the people of Chechnya are ever-more exposed to brutal violations. As China joins the US coalition, the people of Tibet will become less of an "official" concern for the US government.

Security Through Clean Energy: Oil plays a central role in the Middle East. And access to oil has defined US foreign policy and national security interests in the region since the end of World War II. But our dependence on Middle Eastern oil and therefore our seemingly inextricable entanglement in the region is increasingly proving to be a liability...

On top of this add the local pollution and human rights impacts of oil production, transportation and refining, and it makes absolute sense to argue that in order to achieve local and global security in the medium to long term the US needs to rid itself of its dependence on fossil fuels and extract itself from the Middle East quagmire. Such a move would go a long way toward addressing a series of other oil-related human rights and environmental debacles in countries like Nigeria, Ecuador and Indonesia, as well as here at home in places like Louisiana and Los Angeles.

So, despite the fact that we've got a couple of oil men in the White House, the time is ripe for the movement for a different kind of globalization to join hands with environmentalists and peace activists to step up their advocacy for clean energy.

Grassroots Globalization: Finally, the movement against corporate-driven globalization needs to keep doing what it's been doing. Now more than ever, it is important to demonstrate how institutions like the WTO, or trade agreements like NAFTA and the FTAA are letting corporations run rampant across the earth, with little or no regard for local communities, national governments, the environment or human rights. It is essential to continue to show how such a system is deepening poverty and inequality, while potentially leading to greater cultural polarization, religious fundamentalism, and political instability...

"The shock of the horrendous crimes has already opened even elite sectors to reflection of a kind that would have been hard to imagine not long ago, and among the general public that is even more true. Of course, there will be those who demand silent obedience. But it is important not to be intimidated by hysterical ranting and lies and to keep as closely as one can to the course of truth and honesty and concern for the human consequences of what one does, or fails to do."

- Noam Chomsky

All of these efforts will contribute to a more truly secure and healthy globe. In these bleak times, with what may be even darker clouds gathering on the horizon, above all we must continue to believe that, as the slogan of the World Social Forum, held earlier this year in Brazil, declared "another world is possible." And we must continue to build that world.

THIRD WORLD WITHIN -
PEACE ACTION COALITION GUIDING PRINCIPLES

COMPASSION AND MOURNING FOR LIVES LOST

We must demonstrate compassion for the tremendous loss of lives in New York City, Washington D.C., and Pennsylvania from the events of September 11th. We must support families and communities, particularly immigrant, working class and people of color communities in NYC and Washington, DC. Relief must be made available to all who were injured or lost loved ones on September 11th, regardless of immigrant status, marital status (including lesbian, gay, bisexual, transgender families), national origin, and other factors that are used to discriminate.

157

© Margarita Garcia 2001

RESISTING RACIAL/XENOPHOBIC BACKLASH

We can not ignore the thousands of reported (and unreported) incidents of racial violence against people of color in the US, particularly those of/perceived to be of Arab, South Asian, Central Asian descent and/or of Muslim faith. Furthermore, racial profiling – along with surveillance, arbitrary arrest, incarceration and indefinite detention – have been re-accepted by mainstream America, as INS detention centers are being readied as modern-day internment camps. More lives are being lost in this climate of fear and hatred.

SAFETY AND PEACE ARE NOT POSSIBLE WITHOUT RACIAL AND ECONOMIC JUSTICE
We, Third World peoples within and outside of the US, have lived without safety
and peace for years preceding September 11th. This is the time to redefine our
collective understanding of safety and peace to ensure that it is shared
amongst all, and includes freedom from all types of violence (including racial,
economic and other forms), not just physical violence. We recognize that many
who were unsafe before September 11th continue to be under attack in these
times, whether immigrants, communities of color, women, youth, poor and
working-class people, LGBT peoples, or others who oppose institutionalized
oppressions. Current government-sponsored attacks on civil liberties and
increased criminalization/militarization of our communities will be felt most
deeply by communities of color, which have historically borne the brunt of state
violence. We believe that safety and peace will not be real until all of us
are safe.

SOLIDARITY IN A CALL FOR PEACE WITH JUSTICE
We, as communities of color, see it as our obligation to hold the US

government accountable for its actions, carried out in the name of people who
reside in the US. We believe we must unite with other justice-loving people in
this country, and stand in solidarity with those around the world calling for
peace and an end to US-sponsored military and economic retaliation (past &
present) against Third World nations and their peoples.

NO MORE LOST LIVES!
For all these reasons, TWW calls for an end to violence and No More Lost
Lives. If we are serious about creating safety, it can only come about through
peace and justice, not just for ourselves but also for the world community.
More and more, our world is connected. It is crucial that the ties that bind us
are fair and productive for all, not just a few.

Third World Within - Peace Action Coalition, www.nomorelostlives.org

---

7. all day, across the river, the smell of burning rubber and limbs
floats through. the sirens have stopped now. the advertisers are
back on the air. the rescue workers are traumatized. the skyline is
brought back to human size. no longer taunting the gods with its
height.
i have not cried at all while writing this. i cried when i saw those

buildings collapse on themselves like a broken heart. i have never
owned pain that needs to spread like that. and i cry daily that my
brothers return to our mother safe and whole.

there is no poetry in this. there are causes and effects. there are
symbols and ideologies. mad conspiracy here, and information we will
never know. there is death here, and there are promises of more.

there is life here. anyone reading this is breathing, maybe hurting,
but breathing for sure. and if there is any light to come, it will
shine from the eyes of those who look for peace and justice after the
rubble and rhetoric are cleared and the phoenix has risen.

affirm life.

affirm life.

we got to carry each other now.

you are either with life, or against it.

affirm life.

– Suheir Hammad, "First Writing Since"

ORGANIZING THE DISAPPEARED
Pete Diaz, The Funding Exchange

There are thousands of untold stories that will never make it to the attention of
the mainstream media after the devastating events of September 11. Like the
stories of the staff and volunteers of Asociación Tepeyac de New York
(www.tepeyac.org) who have been working non-stop since 9/11. Tepayac's
stated mission is to promote the social welfare and human rights of Mexican
immigrants, specifically the undocumented in New York City. It organizes,
informs and educates immigrants and their families about their rights and
resources. Asociación Tepeyac has had to put all of the community building
work they normally do on hold to deal with the incredible task of organizing
around the issue of undocumented workers who are still missing from the
World Trade Center disaster. "The phones that are still working are always
ringing and we have to deal with everything from families calling in from Latin
America asking about missing relatives, to the Consulates forwarding the

names of families and of the people they think may be missing. Everything else is on hold – English classes, AIDS awareness, community programs," explains Tepeyac's Director, Joel Magallan Reyes. Hundreds of undocumented workers were employed in and around the WTC area. Many of the cooks, busboys and delivery people were undocumented workers from countries like Mexico, Guatemala, Colombia, Honduras, Ecuador, and Nicaragua.

Tepayac is working on two levels to provide emergency help for the victims, families, and friends of the disappeared. First, The Red Cross is working with Tepeyac to identify and list missing workers. Second, Tepayac is organizing undocumented workers now left jobless. They are assisting the newly-unemployed to inform each other of different jobs and opportunities. In some cases, they give advice on how to return to their countries of origin without proper identification. "Flying is out of the question for most, and the train and buses are becoming increasingly more difficult," Joel explains.

The situation at the border is even more dangerous. White ranchers are taking advantage of this time of heightened tension and xenophobia to shoot anything or anyone that moves near the border. Undocumented people returning to the US or Mexico via traditional underground border crossings are being harassed, shot at or taken into custody. Unemployed families who want to return to their country of origin feel trapped in the US. Staying in the US may leave some families homeless while returning may mean death at the border.

The organization seems almost overwhelmed by the present crisis. Their 14th St office is buzzing with people answering phones and interviewing workers affected by the terrorist attacks. Just trying to name the people that worked in or around the WTC is a daunting task; undocumented workers often cannot reveal their real names, and it is rare that employers ask for last names. The web of undocumented employees is being literally mapped out in the main office and hallways of the association. The constant flow of people coming and leaving the office is staggering. The main hallway is full of chairs with people waiting to speak to a volunteer. Some leave happy, informed that a friend or coworker is fine. Others come to ask about missing friends and receive no answers. In spite of all this and working non-stop since the morning of September 11th, the staff at Tepeyac remain upbeat, committed, and optimistic.

Los Capuchinos, prison for 'illegal' immigrants
© Sebastião Salgado, Malaga, Spain, 1997.

To: Jeremy Glick
From: Jee Kim
Subject: Future possibilities

Jeremy,

how are you kid? Darryl mentioned you had a memorial
service for your father last week. Again man, my deepest
condolescences. And all your emails have definitely been
inspiration for me, reminded me of those 2 latino
parents who lost a son but opposed the use of his death
by the gov't to further US terrorism abroad.

has darryl or anyone mentioned to you the project that
me and the folks at Active Element are working on? We're
putting together a collection of writings about Sept 11
to publish as a book with a strong, progressive peace
message. I was wondering if you were interested in doing
any follow up writing about this whole process for you,
the perspective of a young activist directly effected by
all this would be invaluable for the book. let me know,
soon, if possible. Thanks.

stay up,
Jee

acknowledgements

First and foremost, thank you to all the people who contributed to this anthology with their words:

Elsa Mora, Usman Farman, James Creedon, Kiini Ibura Salaam, Suheir Hammad, Kenny Bruno, W. H. Auden, Elizabeth Price, Barbara Kingsolver, Kathleen Pequeo, Georgina Silby, Phyllis and Orlando Rodriguez, Barbara Lee, David Potorti, The National Council of Churches, Amber Amundson, David R. Loy, Greg Nees, The Buddhist Peace Fellowship, Davey D, Danny Hoch, The Coup, Revolutionary Association of the Women of Afghanistan, Tim Wise, Angela Y. Davis, Mark Wilkinson, Robert Scheer, Noam Chomsky, Drummond Pike, Edward Said, Stephen Zunes, Arundhati Roy, Manas Chakravarty, John Maxwell, Larry Mosqueda, Steven Feuerstein, Robert Bowman, Ras Baraka, Eduardo Galeano, Ted Rall, Fidel Castro, Phyllis Bennis, Frank del Olmo, Norman Solomon, Micheal Moore, Russell Mokhiber and Robert Weissman, Chris Buckley, William Hartung, Bill McKibben, Purvi Shah, George Monbiot, Juan Pablo, Pamela J. Podger, John Conyers Jr., Nadia Maiwandi, Michael Gerber and Jonathan Schwarz, The editors of *Rock & Rap Confidential*, Jeff Chang, Duncan Campbell, Jacob Levich, Vandana Shiva, Thich Nhat Hanh, Vicki Robin, Deepak Chopra, Joyce Haboucha, Nina Utne, Paulette Cole, John Robbins, Bishop Desmond Tutu, S. Brian Willson, Amy Cirincione, Dr. Martin Luther King Jr., Cynthia Peters, John Sellers, Bob Wing, Alisa Gravitz, Joshua Karliner, Third World Within, and Pete Diaz.

And to all the folks who blessed this collection with their photographs, illustrations, and artwork:

Jan Blankenstein/Stichting Photo, Nick Cooper, Julie Downey, Carlo Garcia, David Hanks/Global Exchange, Sophia Eminence, David Katz, Daniel Massey, Aaron Mcgruder, Lina Palotta, Dustin Ross, Michel de Ruiter, Sebastião Salgado, Ruben Shafer, Margarita Garcia, Amy Woloszyn, and Richard Yeh.

A special thank you to New Mouth from the Dirty South, Subway and Elevated Press, and The Active Element Foundation and its Peaceful Action Initiative (www.activelement.org).

Billy thanks Jeff Hull, Sara Zia Ebrahimi, Kofi Taha, Gita Drury, Jamie Schweser, Abram Himmelstein and the folks at New Mouth from the Dirty South, Daniel Liao, Margarita Garcia, Mahea Campbell, Amy Cirincione, Adam Hurter, Deepa Fernandes and We Interrupt This Message, David Jacobs, Adam Rice and the folks at Randomwalks, the group that meets at Charas, The Brecht Forum, The Social Venture Network, Solidarity in the Bay, AWOL Magazine, The Active Element Foundation, The Self Education Foundation, Adventure Philanthropy, Colin Greer, Hermon Getatchew, Ibrahim Abdul-Matin, Pablo Caraballo, the Independent Media Center, Manuela Arciniegas, and Adam Mansbach

Margarita thanks Billy for being a catalyst, her cuzin Carlo 'Miko' Garcia for thinking *Bomb the Suburbs* was cool and making art at the last minute. Muito obrigada a Sebastião Salgado for inspiring me to take up my camera again, all the photographers who responded to my pleas for art with generosity – this book would not be half as beautiful without your work. Jee and Amy for your energy and patience with my 'salty' humor, and Daniel Liao without whose endless love, support, and last minute errands I'd be lost.

Amy's acknowledgments: thanks and love to my family and friends for always supporting me. Jee, Margarita, and Billy - so wonderful and energizing to work with. And thanks to BitFlip for letting us work the night shift to finish this project.

Jee thanks, first and foremost, Billiam Upski - for pushing me constantly, Amy – talented, committed, tireless, patient, and funny, and Margarita. We did it. All the dope activists that make me motivate: Ai-Jen, Gina, CAAAV, TWW, Active Element, Stress alumni (esp newswire Kym). The gods: Donnie and Yah (ni**as know). And fam: Amarilis (ok ma, and?), brother Gabe, sister Soups, cousin Leans, cousin Mallie, cousin Moto, Jee Mee, mom and dad, ohm-ma and ah-bah.

Walidah thanks Nadia, Turiya, Ridwan, Andi, Mario and the MOVE family, Kevin and all my AWOL peeps, DJ Cost Effective (aka Ian) and the Neosapien crew, Noah, Bayla, Joy, Petey, Bryonn and Blackout Arts Collective, Brainiac (aka Raymond), Maroon Shoatz, Sundiata Acoli, Rob Thaxton, Fred Hampton Jr. and all political prisoners, and all the many people whose conversations and words have felt my soul, enlightened my mind, kept me sane, and given me hope.

Beka thanks the clan Economopouli, Rainforest Action Network, Flux Factory, Rami El-Assir, Mark Read, David and Jene, Ruckus, the RTS crew, Justin Ruben, Dave Kraft, Celia Alario, the Brownsteins, Ilyse Hogue, Patrick Reinsborough, Quito and Petchuka (#7).

Luis shouts out: mi familia: Maria Elena, Jose, Jose Jr., Maricela, Gabriel, Elisa, Nicolas, Gabriel, Marco, mama chuy, y todas mis tias y tios. All YOC (San Diego and LA), Olin (Oakland and Frisco), and InnerCity Struggle organizers. All the SNJ crew. SNJ statewide network: SCYEA, Youth-EJ, TEM415, Still We Rise, Wise Up. To all the rest of the homies that kept me real. Remember: when organizers become participants, people die! Free Palestine. Viva los Zapatistas. End all economic apartheid and long live a free South Africa. Long live a revolutionary society free of sexism, homophobia, racism, capitalism, imperialism, and Zionism. Check out: www.schoolsnotjails.com.

Shaffy acknowledges the efforts of UC Berkeley's Students for Justice in Palestine and all similar student groups across the country. Thank you to Mike Rubio, Outreach Coordinator of Youth Radio and all people who work in prisons and with young people who routinely don't get any breaks. And thanks to my family, who taught me to care about all this stuff in the first place.

Jeremy thanks the Blu Collective, the Baraka Family, *Unity and Struggle*, Black NIA Force, Darryl, Dax, Boots Riley, Mike Crockford, The Ramah Folk in the kitchen and out, Mario Africa and the MOVE family, *AWOL*, Vee, russell shoatz III, Suheir and Lilly for the calls, Edgar Rivera Colon, Wesley Brown, Mike Ladd for the kind holler, Heidi, Jeff Garris and PA Abolitionists, Bud Welch, Mike Rubenstein, the great Brent Edwards, Jee and Active Element for holding down a project like this, Elaine and Brian, my family – sister, mom, and dad, Barry H. Glick. New Brunswick, Newark, New York soldiers. All revolutionaries all over the world.

resources

News and essays:

www.zmag.org

www.commondreams.org

www.tompaine.com

www.alternet.org

www.randomwalks.com

For information on how the media distorts the news: www.fair.org

For excellent links on the Middle East: www.al-awda.org/newyork/links.html

Analysis of US foreign policy:

www.wtc.blogspot.com

www.blowback.blogspot.com

www.killyourtv.com/wartime

www.nyc.indymedia.org

www.monkeyfist.com

www.poynter.org

www.guardian.co.uk

Manufacturing Consent: The Political Economy of the Mass Media, Noam Chomsky

Fateful Triangle: The United States, Israel and the Palestinians, Noam Chomsky

Listings and information:

www.rawasongs.fancymarketing.net/index.html: Revolutionary Association of the Women of Afghanistan

www.saja.org/roundupsept11.html: South Asian Journalists Association

www.schoolsnotjails.com: Los Angeles-based youth network

Ways to get involved:

www.9-11peace.org: The biggest 9/11 peace petition site on the web - started by a 20 year old from Boston, it has received more than a million visits.

www.teachingforchange.org/sept11.htm: An excellent resource for teachers.

www.peacefuljustice.cjb.net: Based at Wesleyan University, a major nerve center for student anti-war organizing.

www.adc.org: The American-Arab Anti-Discrimination Committee. Please call to report any incidents (202) 244-2990.

www.911peace.net: 911 Peace Network, action for justice and peace

www.antiwar.com

www.pax.protest.net: Action news and calendar

www.nowarcollective.com: No War Collective Crisis Resource Center

www.saveageneration.org: Education for Peace in Iraq Center

www.nynotinourname.org: New York Not In Our Name: "Our grief is not a cry for war"

www.nomorelostlives.org: Third World Within – Peace Action Coalition, NYC

www.geocities.com/catcruz: Bay Area (Ca.) peace events

www.gatheringofhope.org: Emerging international peace network

about the editors

Born in Korea and raised in Philly, **Jee Kim** has called New York home since 1991. An activist, writer, and new media consultant, Jee has served as senior editor at *Stress* Magazine and currently works with Violator, Active Element, and CAAAV. He received his academic training from Columbia and Oxford Universities, which has been mysteriously funneled into his core passions: alternative media, Hip Hop, and the struggles of urban youth of color.

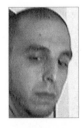

Jeremy M. Glick is a 5th year graduate student in Afro-American Literature and Revolutionary Theory at Rutgers University. He has written for *Stress* and *Blu* magazines and is on the editorial board of *Unity and Struggle* with Amiri Baraka, among others. He is involved in various activist campaigns pertaining to justice for political prisoners, anti-imperialist organizations, the death penalty, and police brutality. He teaches at Rutgers and NYU, sometimes.

Shaffy Moeel, 22, was in a cafe in South Africa with a friend on September 11 when news of the World Trade Center attack came on TV. Everyone immediately surrounded them and wanted to know what they felt, as Americans. She returned to Berkeley to find that as an Iranian and Turk, she was suddenly more "Other" than ever. A former reporter for Youth Radio (and past contributor to NPR), Shaffy works with young people in prison and with Students for Justice in Palestine at UC Berkeley where she recently graduated with a degree in Peace and Conflict Studies.

Born and raised in Los Angeles, **Luis Antonio Sanchez**, 27, is a writer, video and media activist, and community organizer. He is a founder of Youth Organizing Communities, which has been at the forefront of California's statewide Schools Not Jails/Students Not Soldiers movement, demanding educational justice and an end to both the prison-industrial and the military-industrial complex. A graduate of UC Berkeley in English, he currently works at InnerCity Struggle in East Los Angeles as the director of youth programs.

Beka Economopoulos, 27, has been a creative leader in the environmental and anti-globalization movements. She is a trainer for the Ruckus Society and was the East Coast Organizer for the Rainforest Action Network, spearheading their campaign against Citigroup, "The World's Most Destructive Bank." She coordinated media for the protests at the Republican convention in Philadelphia and was involved with the mobilizations in Seattle and Washington, DC. In 1999 she organized the ECOnference, the largest student environmental gathering in 10 years.

Walidah Imarisha is a 22 year old Black woman who grew up on military bases, attended college in Portland until she got tired of what she calls "translation activism" ("I got tired of having to translate everything for white people") and moved to North Philly to work on prison, globalization, and military issues with AWOL magazine and International Friends and Family of Mumia Abu Jamal. A spoken word artist, poet, essayist, journalist, historian, and general rabble-rouser, Walidah Imarisha is the author of *children of ex-slaves: the unfinished revolution*. She is the bad sista part of the dynamic poetry duo Good Sista/Bad Sista, with her better half, Turiya Autry.

167

THE DESIGNER
Amy Woloszyn, a Pratt Institute graduate with a degree in Communication Design, has been applying her passion for design to a variety of fields for the past four years. She has gained experience in print and web design through working in film, theater, music, and media. *Another World is Possible* is this 23 year old's first project in political activism but by no means her last.

THE PHOTO EDITOR
Born on the South Side of Chicago, **Margarita Garcia** began her photographic career at 16, publishing in *The Source* and *Bomb the Suburbs*. Her photos published in the Chicago Reader were nominated for Best Article (1992) by the Chicago Press Association. After a 10 year hiatus as an activist, capoerista, poet, and project manager, her work for the "What's Your Anti-Drug?" campaign won a Bronze Lion award at the 2001 Cannes Advertising festival. She currently resides in Queens, New York.

publisher's note

A Conversation Sparking Campaign... Disguised as a Book

With a December 11 release date, this book sticks its neck out as the first major progressive, literary response to September 11th. But this isn't just a book. It's a conversation sparking campaign. We want to invite you to spark with us. Carry the book around with you. Read it in public. Leave it in your bathroom when guests come over. People are going to ask you: "What's that book about?" Buy a copy for your uncle who has a flag flying from both sides of his SUV. Buy ten copies directly from our distributor (www.newmouthfromthedirtysouth.com) for 50% off (see copyright page). Order 50 copies and sell them out of your bag at anti-war rallies and Hip Hop events. Put up stickers and posters. Start a book group. See, it's not just a book to spark idle conversations. It's a book that raises the questions: "What can we do?" "What can EACH of us do?" That's why instead of one author, we recruited an all-star team of SIX energetic editors from diverse movements across the country. They came together magically. With no budget, they did six months of work in the space of six weeks. All six are planning to tour the book, as their schedules permit, for a significant portion of the next year and perhaps beyond. All six are brilliant at sparking conversations; they can help you use the book as a conversation-sparking device. We expect to help generate hundreds of hope-inspiring events in more than 50 cities across the US and to strengthen, sharpen, and diversify the emerging anti-war movement while connecting it to ongoing local efforts. College speaking fees will pay the travel bill for this extensive national field organizing campaign. So if you're connected to a college, school, organization, or bookstore, please visit www.anotherworldispossible.net. Drop us a line and invite Shaffy, Luis, Jeremy, Jee, Beka or Walidah to come spark conversations with you.

William "Upski" Wimsatt
Publisher, Subway & Elevated Press